The Careful vs. The Careless Driver

Driver Expertise
By
Chaz Van Heyden - Chauffeur

Book I: The Careful (Predictive Driver)

Book II: The Careless Driver
(The Undertrained Driver)

VG Publishing
Nashville, Tenn

© 2020, 2022

ALL RIGHTS RESERVED

Printed in The United States

Reviews

"Van Heyden does a marvelous job with *The Careless Driver* of making us think in regards to the state of our driving in today's society. With an obvious disregard to others on the roadway, we have forgotten the common courtesy of the system. It's amazing to me to see, through interview, how our education has altered over the years. This is a book that is needed in the hands of all potential licensees."
John Blanks (Technical Sales for Tesla)

"An interesting read for people learning to drive. It's a book that is a good reference text that will be most beneficial to be ear marked and reread many times. Loaded with solid information for drivers of all ages. This book should be made available to students at all driving schools. If it prevents even one fatality on the roadways, then Mr. Van Heyden made a huge accomplishment here. Add this one to your library, give one to a friend learning to drive, make highways safer. Congrats on another fine endeavor" F. Botham (Author)

"I really enjoyed *The Careless Driver*. The author does a good job of getting multiple perspectives on driving education or lack thereof and sheds light on some of the flaws in the American driver education system. The book has large text and is easy to read." C. Moore (Banking Officer)

I was very curious about the book and its contents, and I was very pleased to see that someone else noticed some of the strange driving behaviors out on the road. It was news to me how little education there really is for new drivers. You can kind of tell if you spend any time on the road some of these behaviors could be prevented with enough knowledge and teaching, and some of the normal behaviors of driving on the road. I agree with the conclusions in the book, especially hands-on experience is always the best. If [state] legislators get copies of this book there is a chance they will introduce bills along the lines recommended in *The Careless Driver.* It would be a good direction to go. Brandon Williams Business Owner

DEDICATED TO THE DRIVERS
WHO DID GET TRAINED
ADEQUATELY

Contents

Preface   **11**
Expertise #1 No prediction vs. looking ahead   13
Expertise #2 Space between cars   17
Expertise #3 Night driving   21
Expertise #4 A skill called 'pacing'   23
Expertise #5 Do you *have to* commute?   27
Expertise #6 Trucks & Heavy Equipment   31
Expertise #7 The most basic expertise   33
Expertise #8 To Yield or not to Yield   35
Expertise #9 Utilizing your car's gears.   37
Expertise #10 Arguments in the car   39
Expertise #11 Skids   47
Expertise #12 The Golden Rule Chapter   49
Safeguarding Your Chances of Getting Hit.   61
Rationale for Handling DUI & Repeat Offenders 63

Book II <u>The Careless Driver</u> Table of Contents   1
Legislation currently introduced   135
Appendix

The Careful vs. The Careless Driver

Publishers Note:

It is recommended that this work is read through in one sitting *swiftly* looking for information that is real or that one has experienced. Then, re-read the entire work *for blood*.

Also note, that as this edition 2022 is published the rate of 2021 U.S. roadway fatalities is at the halfway point of the year 18% above 2020. Further, even though "NHTSA projects that the second quarter of 2022, from April to June, had the first decline in fatalities after seven consecutive quarters of year-to-year increases in fatalities that began in the third quarter of 2020. they are still at high levels that call for urgent and sustained action."

The material in this book was gathered from motorists in the United States of America, however, it would easily fulfill its missions with other countries since 1.3 million lives are lost each year worldwide from motor vehicle collisions with other motor vehicles, pedestrians and animals.

Preface

I have chauffeured thousands of individuals. And, while doing so have had the opportunity to drive in all types of weather, roads and traffic conditions, seeing all types of driver *driving* weaknesses and errors. The purpose of this book's writing is not only to reduce the number of roadway fatalities significantly, but also provide a pathway to a much less stressful driving environment for drivers which otherwise in no small part contributes to hasty actions and misjudgments while driving.

In the earlier book <u>The Careless Driver,</u> (book II) the author interviewed, researched, recorded and then published findings from 26 driver's driving skill histories along with professional level observations about driver's driving habits and errors. This book covers some of the misinformation and unskilled maneuvers they related in those interviews but provides for comparison expert methods of dealing with traffic situations that can or will replace those habits and errors with greater chances in improved driving conditions for all drivers.

The Careful vs. The Careless Driver

A note here as to format: <u>I have chosen to CAPITALIZE all the 'expertise' so that they are received by the reader with more weight than the running narrative.</u>

Awareness alone is not sufficient to keep one's vehicle from colliding with another vehicle, persons or animals. It takes driver expertise in looking at patterns in traffic, knowing alternate routes well enough to quickly and accurately take the better, not necessarily the faster, safer route, and it takes *<u>heightened awareness of road and traffic conditions.</u>*

No Prediction vs. Looking Ahead

(Expertise #1)

First, let's discuss patterns of traffic: the 'rush hour' as we know it is called but in truth it is the 'snail hour' just as postal mail has incurred the moniker 'snail mail' in contrast to "e" mail.

Rush hour is when the fun really begins, and I am entirely sarcastic when I say fun. Because death and disfigurement are no fun to anyone, even the few evil-intentioned. We go through the same scenario workday by workday and yet we see 'no change' in the congestion. Why? The reason is no mystery when we look at what causes the congestion, even with including unexpected construction crews on our way to and from work. That's the keyword, *unexpected*. *But,* with expertise about traffic patterns these *unexpected* factors become *predictable factors* and can thereby surrender to the *alternate route remedy or the sooner than later lane changes necessary to go by the construction crews without having to slow to a crawl.* Again, this is one of many scenarios. This 'predictable factor' includes where two major Interstates merge.
So, if we are traveling as many of us do to work on an eight-lane Interstate (four lanes one-way), or at minimum six lanes, we know that 99% of traffic

The Careful vs. The Careless Driver

entering the Interstate enters from the right lane through merging, as we move along, <u>and</u> we know that heavy trucks take the longest to get up to speed, and sometimes just barge into the passenger car lanes regardless. We know this because <u>we have seen it happen many times.</u> (See illustration A1)

We will include many 'senior drivers' also who are tentative drivers and tend to drive onto Interstates slower than we would. These seniors drive slower than the right most lane traffic is going and cause that lane to slow up and start a chain reaction behind with cars <u>not predicting this scenario, and</u> to cause them immediately to change lanes to the detriment of the drivers of the lane to their left. We can call this the 'escape maneuver'-- and that is also a symptom of what?

The *no prediction factor* of non-expert driving. But lesser in weight than the right-hand lane drivers who blindly *don't see* and *do not predict* the senior driver, lumbering 18-wheeler, or heavy construction vehicle scenario.

Ill. A1

The Careful vs. The Careless Driver

Many times, there won't be signs like this (especially on Interstate roads going through a city) to take note of ahead of the incident.

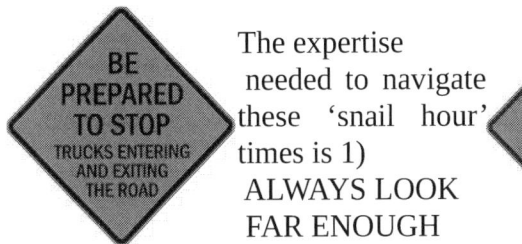

The expertise needed to navigate these 'snail hour' times is 1) ALWAYS LOOK FAR ENOUGH AHEAD WHILE DRIVING SO AS NOT TO BE CONSTANTLY CROWDING UP BEHIND OR COMING UP ON THE BACK OF ANOTHER VEHICLE AND **HAVING TO PUT ON THE BRAKES.** *THIS IS ESPECIALLY REQUIRED OF SUV's since the forward momentum is twice to three times that of a standard passenger car.* Did you know that the weight of a Nissan *Armada* is twice that of a Nissan *Altima?* The Chevy Avalanche is 7,000 to 7,200 lbs gross weight vs. Chevy Impala, 3600 to 3800 lbs. But, of course looking far enough ahead means there will be less *emergency braking,* which translates into fewer 'brake jobs', and won't that be a terrible blow to our U.S. economy? (See, sarcasm again.)

Also, in several major cities a motorist can look, *before they set out to drive,* at a *heat map* of the highways that show the relative volume of traffic on major routes and some mapping devices will show road closures and construction in progress. *Waze* is one such app that does so on a mobile phone.

The Careful vs. The Careless Driver

Space Between Cars

Expertise #2

SIMPLY LETTING THE CAR AHEAD OR TRUCK GET AHEAD TWO OR THREE *EXTRA CAR LENGTHS* ALLOWS THE VEHICLE YOU ARE DRIVING TO SLOW DOWN SUFFICIENTLY IN MOST CASES TO CONTINUE *WITHOUT HAVING TO BRAKE.* Did you know that TESLA engineered 'let off the gas' auto-braking that acts more like a brake? Works fabulously well.

Now, let's delve into ALTERNATE ROUTES <u>*TO WORK.*</u> (We can always prep for an excursion or vacation beforehand in a timely manner.) Yeah, that 'alternate route'... Well, if you haven't taken it at least one time you will DEFINITELY NOT TAKE IT AS AN ALTERNATE ROUTE TO WORK WHEN THE 'SNAIL HOUR' HITS. <u>WE HAVE TO EXPERIMENT.</u> AND THE BEST TIME TO EXPERIMENT IS ON THE WEEKEND! NOT WHEN GETTING TO WORK <u>LATE,</u> IS GOING TO COST US OUR JOBS OR A 'BOSS INTERVIEW'. Find two or three alternate routes that satisfy, and please don't argue that it is a longer route. Longer, but faster by a factor of 2 to 10Xs the snail route. Plus, it is A LOT LESS STRESSFUL KNOWING THAT FEWER MOTORISTS WILL BE DOING THIS ALSO, AS YOU ARE. MOST LIKELY

ONLY THE 'EXPERT DRIVERS' AS YOU HAVE NOW BECOME.

In fact, I do not let my driving speed be influenced by anyone or any idea some other driver tries to put into my head. If the speed limit is 70 MPH, DO I HAVE TO TRAVEL AT 70 MILES PER HOUR? THE HELL I DO. That's the posted legal limit—remember the golden rule (prima facie rule), all law enforcement officers do: Are you driving at a safe speed? By traveling at 65 mph (remember when that was the highest you could go?) I hang back like a wise ranch-hand to see how and which way the steers are gonna head. (That's the cowboy part in me.)

And for the love of Hubbard, add a few extra minutes to the commute time and that alone will suffice to allow for driving at your designated speed, NOT WHAT IS EVERY OTHER DRIVER'S SPEED. Of course, if you do elect to travel at 65 or 60 mph <u>please drive in the farthest to the right lane</u>. That's expected and in many states is a traffic law, citable by the way. Note: Have you taken stock of how many crashes occur in the two fastest lanes? Check up on the data and you'll find if you haven't noticed that's where the deadliest crashes occur.

While we are speaking on the subject of alternate routes let's take up the all too common example on city streets of a motorists trying to get across 4 or 6 lanes in heavy traffic coming out of a gas station or shopping center. Instead of causing untold consternation with drivers streaming in front, and to avoid stress and a potential serious collision, instead of trying to maneuver through the dense traffic or when traffic is halted at the light, take an easy right into the first lane and guide the vehicle over to the left-hand most lane to make a U-Turn at the closest light. <u>Even if there is a "No U-Turn" at that intersection, proceed left anyway and navigate to a near driveway to perform another safe and easy left turn and get back to the intersection for a right turn.</u> It's not just an 'artful' method of driving, it takes into consideration all drivers and the responsibilities of an expert driver to minimize conditions that lead to <u>unnecessary collisions</u>.

Can't speak for anyone else so I'll go on record: I love to speed, to travel fast, even faster than the posted speed limit when TRAFFIC CONDITIONS WARRANT IT. But I get off just as fine doing my 65 MPH in the far-right lane enjoying the blooming fun outa life just as much cruisin' the same way when I'm taking a leisure vacation out west with all the time in the world.

All right we have taken a good look at traffic patterns and alternate routes, but not all yet. What we know now about Interstate driving during *snail hours* can and should be applied to city and country road driving. If we know where the school districts are, or mainly know, we won't run afoul of them when we take *the alternate route* along non-Interstate roadways. We also need to know which city streets are good alternates from the usual to get from work to the Interstate. The only way I know is to experiment, and to explore other routes in your city. You will no doubt find that at certain hours Monday through Friday certain arteries (love that term) are ALWAYS FULL OF COMMUTERS HEADING TO WORK!

BUT WE DON'T WANT (AS EXPERT DRIVERS) TO HAVE TO ALWAYS BE IN THAT TRAFFIC SCENARIO, DO WE?

AND AS WITH INTERSTATES THERE ARE MOST ALWAYS CONSTRUCTION CREWS AT WORK IN OUR CITIES.

Now, it is true that we have the glorious 21st-century tool we know as GPS. Why not use it? Let's put technology and our super-wise newly found hunger for expertise in driving to take us where we want to go? Do you trust your GPS? I didn't for quite some time. Now I do. It is almost 100% correct each time I use it. Some brands of GPS tell us even where new construction is happening!

Armed with our new understanding of traffic patterns (not all by any means) and the freedom to choose the speed our vehicles 'mobilate' forward with, and our savvy of alternate routes, we are well on our way to expert, carefree driving instead of careless driving and *stressful* driving.

More *simple* expertise points:

Night Driving

Expertise # 3

AT NIGHT ON 2-LANE COUNTY AND COUNTRY ROADS WHEN THE ONCOMING LIGHTS ARE SEVERAL AND CONTINUOUS, I TURN ON AN OVERHEAD COMPARTMENT LIGHT AKA COURTESY LIGHT, SOMETIMES BOTH. WHY? BECAUSE THE EXTRA LIGHT NARROWS, I.E. CAUSES THE IRIS OF MY EYES TO CLOSE DOWN MY PUPILS ENOUGH AND THAT REDUCES THE GLARE. WHEREAS I WAS TAUGHT AS SOME OF YOU HAVE BEEN TO LOOK AWAY FROM THE HIGHWAY OVER TO THE SIDE, WHICH IS COURTING DISASTER IN SOME CASES BUT FOR SURE IS LESS EFFECTIVE TO HANDLE THE GLARE, ESPECIALLY WHEN THERE ARE MANY CARS COMING ONE BEHIND THE OTHER.

The Careful vs. The Careless Driver

At night on 2-Lane county and country roads the oncoming headlights are continuous.
I turn on an overhead compartment light (Aka The Courtesy Light)
to minamize the glare of oncoming headlights.

The extra light narrows my pupils and
that reduces the glare from the headlights.

I was taught, as some of you have been; to look away from the highway to the side of the road.
Losing sight of the road courts disaster and is less effective when handling the glare.
Especially, when there are so many cars coming one behind the other.

A Skill Called 'Pacing'

Expertise # 4

ON STATE ROADS I ADJUST MY SPEED SO THAT I AM SLOWING DOWN WELL BEFORE A RED LIGHT SO BY THE TIME I GET TO THE LIGHT IT IS GREEN AND I CAN SMOOTHLY ACCELERATE AND ENJOY NOT HAVING TO STOP AND GO AS A PATTERN OF DRIVING. CONTRARY, I KNOW TOO, AND SEE CONTINUOUSLY OTHER DRIVERS EXHIBIT. THEY GO SAILING UP TO AND STOP AT THE RED LIGHT AND THEN START UP WITHOUT LOOKING AHEAD AND DO THE SAME EXACT MANEUVER JUMPING OFF AT THE GREEN AND GO SAILING TO THE NEXT RED LIGHT AND HAVE TO STOP AGAIN. THE WISE ROAD ENGINEERS, WHO BREATHE THE SAME AIR WE BREATHE, WHO LIVE IN OUR NEIGHBORHOODS WHO TRAVEL THE SAME ROADS WE DO STUDIED AND CAME UP WITH THE OPTIMUM SPEEDS FOR CITY AND STATE ROADS. THEY DID SOME CALM ESTIMATING AND TESTING. WHO AM I TO GAINSAY OR SUPERSEDE THEIR WISDOM? AND SO, I FIND THAT I CAN LITERALLY TRAVEL WITHOUT HAVING TO STOP BUT A SINGLE TIME, MOST OF THE TIME, GOING TO AND COMING FROM LOCAL DESTINATIONS BECAUSE I KNOW FROM OBSERVATION THAT THE LIGHTS ARE TIMED FOR 35 MILES PER HOUR.

The Careful vs. The Careless Driver

As mentioned in *The Careless Driver, edition #1 & 2*, one 3-week period in December 2017 I witnessed 11 different collisions within a 3-mile radius of where I reside. And on Christmas day 2017 there were 7 collisions before the afternoon in the Nashville area, <u>seven</u>. Further I stated in TCD release #1 and #2 edition: *"If there were no or greatly fewer collisions of vehicles there would be no or greatly fewer fatalities on our U.S. highways and roadways. I also stated that no fatalities is unreal and not to be expected even years after this information is applied broadly. Why? Because there is and probably always will be 'pilot error' as I discussed with Mari Mitchell on her broadcast 'Dare To Be Authentic'.* This book is dedicated to those who want to ensure that they never drive a vehicle into another human being, animal or solid object so as to cause injury or death to living organisms.

To accomplish this, it is not enough to drive 'Defensively' since all battles and contests and games are won through a balance of offense (positive, causative actions) and defensive ones. Offensive-- Causative (Predictive) driving is attained through driving expertise. Ex: you are traveling in lane #3 of a 4-lane Interstate (one-way) and you observe ahead, not far ahead—perhaps a hundred to two hundred feet ahead—a driver coming up fast on another vehicle in the #4 or 'exit lane'. You certainly can predict that as you approach the slower lane traffic ahead this driver is going to bolt over into your lane

The Careful vs. The Careless Driver

to get around the driver that is impeding the encroaching driver's advance. I experienced such a maneuver with a paying passenger in the Summer of 2017. This driver was bullying quite blatantly a driver ahead of him in #2 lane and suddenly at 80 mph (I was passing in the #1 lane at about that speed) bolts into my lane and causes me to brake to avoid collision which would have had dire if not deadly consequences. I chased this careless, should I say reckless driver for about a mile and a half to get his license plate number and reported it. I was going to trace the driver and take him to court since my passenger was a witness and willing to go to court as well. This did not occur because I was a few yards short of the Nashville, TN county line requiring that I file in another county than where I lived and at an expense I did not consider was appropriate. I did however predict the driver's careless and *knuckleheaded maneuver.*

At this juncture it may interest many and it is very important as to why I am publishing this book? I differ from a majority of individuals (as I should) in that I consider it is inefficient to grow a bunch of bodies and then destroy them in the most confused and disorganized manner imaginable. It goes against everything I have wanted to achieve in life. Not quite as counter-productive and nuts as waging war against civilians—that usually outnumber military combatants in deaths and mutilation--but a type of war against human life I find is contemptible. I'm talking of course about those who have lost control of their lives to such a degree that they actively wage war against their own survival and unbeknownst to their neighbor's, their neighbor's survival. If a person is bent on destroying their body, that they no longer either trust to survive according to their intentions nor consider it can persist and achieve anything of worth in this life, I say O.K. fine, you want to end it all? But PLEASE DON'T AFFECT TRAFFIC!

We cheapen life when we don't make every effort to understand life and to understand others. To gain any expertise it is going to happen if we first understand life and others.

◆◆◆

Let's go on...

Do You Have To Commute?

Expertise # 5

IF YOU WORK 'DOWNTOWN' OR DOWNTOWN TYPE ENVIRONMENT AND PARK DOWNTOWN AND IT COSTS YOU BEAUCOU BUCKS (LIKE $20 PER DAY) I'D CONSIDER UTILIZING UBER OR LYFT THE WAY SEVERAL RIDERS IN MY VEHICLE WERE DOING WHEN I WAS CHAUFFEURING. THEY TOLD ME IT'S MUCH MORE ECONOMICAL USING THE RIDE-SHARES THAN PAYING THE INSURANCE, FINDING PARKING, THE FUEL AND THE REST OF IT JUST TO THE HAVE ANNOYANCE OF THE TRAFFIC AND THE 100.00 PER WEEK PARKING FEES.

It makes entire sense. Why contribute to the congestion when two or more individuals who work together can Uber or Lyft or Grab to work and back. Cheap, efficient and relaxing to have a professional driver chauffeur us to work. Wow, is that not a concept worth following?

IF ONE WORKS OR CAN WORK FROM HOME, ONE IS ABLE TO ADJUDICATE THE BETTER TIMES TO RUN ERRANDS, MAKE APPOINTMENTS, SEE FRIENDS DURING SLACK TRAFFIC HOURS. YOU KNOW WHEN THESE ARE: 10:00 AM TO 11:45, SKIP LUNCH IF YOU

ARE AROUND METROPOLITAN INTERSTATES. THEN AGAIN 1:15 PM TO ABOUT 3:00 PM AND SKIP THE 'SNAIL HOURS' AS WORKERS POUR OUT OF DOWNTOWN TO GO HOME ON THE INTERSTATE. IF YOU'RE NOT AT HOME EARNING BREAD, WORK CAN BE DONE AT HOME SUCH AS CERTAIN SERVICE JOBS OR QUANTITATIVE JOBS RATHER THAN IN PERSON SERVICE ORIENTED. APPLY TO YOUR HEAD ADMINISTRATOR OR OWNER FOR HOURS THAT ALLOW YOU TO WORK LATER THAN 5:00 PM IN RETURN FOR A DAY OFF FOR FOUR DAYS AT 10 HOURS PER DAY. IT MIGHT TURN OUT BENEFICIAL FOR BOTH.

IF AND WHEN I HAVE TO BE IN DOWNTOWN MONDAY THROUGH FRIDAY AROUND 4:00 OR 5:00 PM AND I DON'T WANT TO DRIVE HOME IN THE MELEE THAT IS CALLED 'RUSH HOUR' WHICH TRUTHFULLY SHOULD BE RENAMED 'SNAIL HOUR'; I CAN CHOOSE SEVERAL OTHER PRE-DETERMINED ACTIVITIES, SUCH AS GOING TO THE LIBRARY AND TAKING OUT A BOOK AND READING FOR TWO HOURS. YOU KNOW, GET SOME ADDITIONAL EDUCATION. OR GO TO A PUB AND HAVE SOME FRIENDLY CONVERSATION OR WATCH SOME SPORTS EVENT THAT I LIKE—CAREFUL NOT TO DRINK MORE THAN ONE BEER, IF I DRINK AT ALL, SO THAT BY TWO HOURS WHEN THE TRAFFIC HAS DIED DOWN MY BLOOD ALCOHOL LEVEL IS NIL AD I CAN DRIVE 100% IN THE PRESENT, ENJOYING A LEISURE, PLEASANT DRIVE HOME.

The Careful vs. The Careless Driver

I CAPITALIZE these points so that they are received with extra weight and they should be received with extra weight since the title of this work is <u>THE CAREFUL DRIVER</u>.

Let's turn our attention to 'unknown' and poorly known dynamics of moving vehicles.

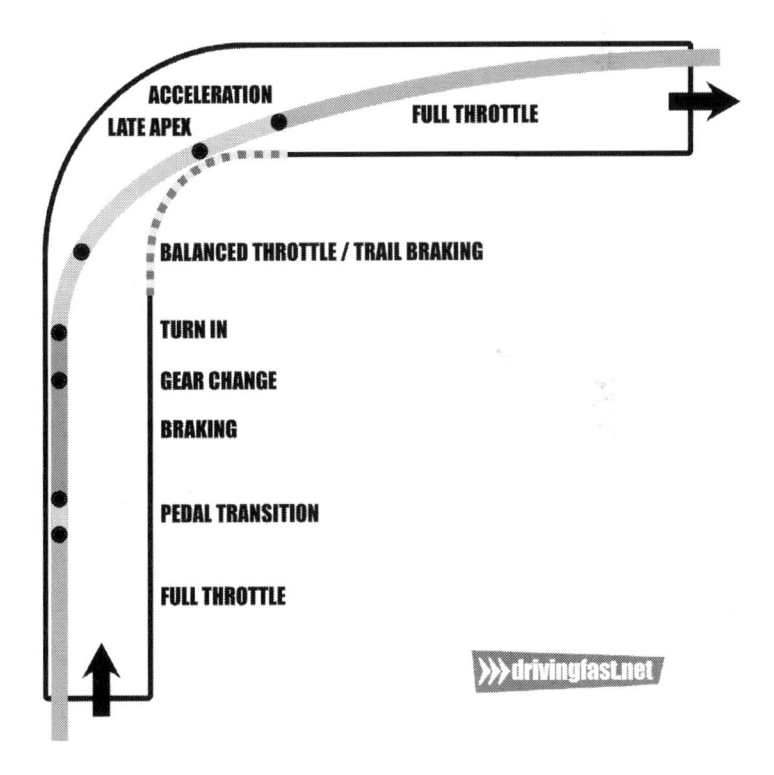

Ill. #1B

```
ACCELERATION
LATE APEX              FULL THROTTLE

BALANCED THROTTLE / TRAIL BRAKING

TURN IN
GEAR CHANGE
BRAKING

PEDAL TRANSITION

FULL THROTTLE
                        »»drivingfast.net
```

When should an expert driver slow down when leaving an Interstate on a severely curving exit, or when taking a 270° turn-off for another Interstate or highway. Well before the turn, NOT INTO OR DURING THE TURN. To do otherwise not only greatly reduces control of the vehicle but it makes passengers slide to the opposite side or at minimum throws their bodies towards the opposite side of the vehicle making for an abrupt and uncomfortable experience: not to mention spilled baby formulas, spilled hot coffee and other beverages as well. A gradual speed up keeps every passenger and the driver upright and pressed gently against the seat back making for a most pleasant experience even on fast turns. These scenarios worsen in damp or rainy weather. Got the idea? In my years as both a chauffeur and a motorist on public highways, the predominant method I see of drivers leaving a highway or Interstate that curves significantly (exit to street or exit to another highway/Interstate) is to brake as they are in the turn. See illustration #1B

If this is how a race car driver handles a 'fast' turn, then we can all learn from an expert driver. And, although most car drivers won't take a turn of 90° or more at speed, the fact that this is possible is worthy of note. I would recommend this method only for an expert driver needing to get to destination "B" from "A" in an Emergency situation or driving alone. The point illustrated though is not taking the turn at speed but at what point is braking necessary to do so. Review diagram.

Trucks & Heavy Equipment

Expertise # 6

REALIZE THAT TRUCKS AND HEAVY EQUIPMENT VEHICLES ARE NEVER GOING TO DISAPPEAR FROM OUR INTERSTATES BECAUSE THEY ARE FEDERAL HIGHWAYS AND LOCAL GOVERNMENT HAS NO JURISDICTION OVER THEM. SO, FIND OUT, OR DISCOVER OR REALIZE AND OBSERVE WHEN THESE TRUCKS ARE USUALLY COMING ONTO THE INTERSTATE AT A SLOW PONDEROUS RATE CAUSING UNALERT RIGHT HAND LANE DRIVERS TO ALMOST COME TO A SCREECHING HALT BECAUSE THEY HAVE NOT MADE THEMSELVES AWARE OF THE FACT THAT THESE LARGE TRUCKS DO THIS DAILY. CAUSING CARS AND LIGHT TRUCKS AND VANS BEHIND TO DART TO THE LEFT SUDDENLY (**SO THEY DON'T HIT OR HAVE TO SLOW DOWN TO PRACTICALLY CRAWLING ON A ROADWAY THAT IS DESIGNED AND BUILT FOR FAST UNIMPEDED FLOWS OF TRAFFIC**). AND CAUSING <u>THAT LANE</u> (THE ONE THEY'RE DARTING INTO) TO SLOW DOWN AND VEHICLES BEHIND TO DART OVER TO THE NEXT LANE AND SO ON TO THE POINT WHERE THE ENTIRE FOUR LANE INTERSTATE COMES TO A STOP! WHICH IS NUTS <u>AND SUPER INEFFICIENT</u> WHEN YOU

The Careful vs. The Careless Driver

CONSIDER IT. THESE LARGE SLOW-MOVING TRUCKS COME ONTO AND INTO THEIR LANE THAT THEY TRAVEL MANY TIMES A WEEK AND AT THE SAME ENTRANCES WITHOUT FAIL. THE MORAL? HERE'S AN ILLUSTRATION OF ONE OF THE SCENARIOS WITH TRUCKS. (Reverse truck's position in diagram with car's position.)

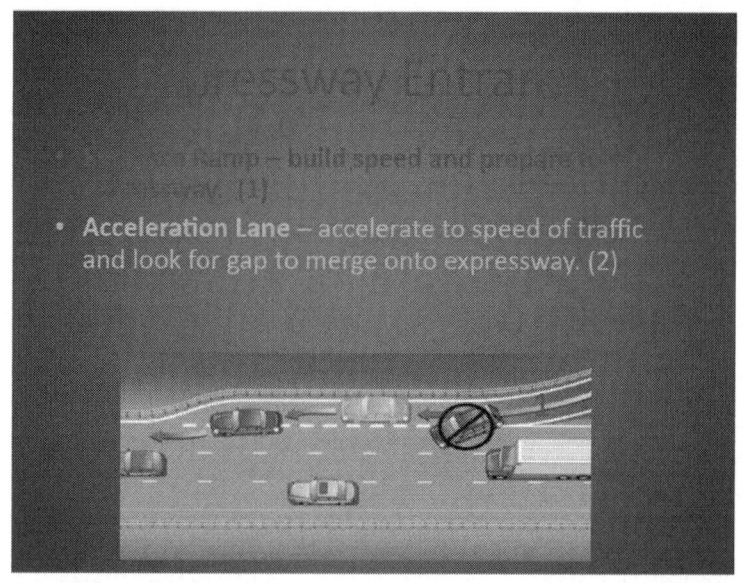

ALWAYS BE LOOKING FAR ENOUGH AHEAD TO SPOT THE INEVITABLE SLOW-DOWN AND TAKE DECISIVE ACTION EARLY ON TO MOVE OVER SMOOTHLY WITH SIGNALING ENOUGH TIMES TO WARN TRAFFIC BEHIND AND AVOID THE WHOLE MESS. Note: in illus. above reverse the tractor-trailer position with the car barging in from the right.

The Most Basic Expertise

Expertise # 7

THE MOST BASIC OF ALL PRINCIPLES I UTILIZE, AND THAT MOST OF US HAVE BEEN AWARE OF ALL OUR LIVES, IS: ALLOW YOURSELF EXTRA TIME TO GET FROM POINT 'A' TO POINT 'B' SO THAT YOU ARE NOT SELF-RUSHING TO AND FROM WORK OR TO AND FROM IMPORTANT APPOINTMENTS CAUSING YOU TO DO THINGS WITH YOUR CAR THAT YOU SHOULDN'T BE DOING.

HAVE YOUR ALTERNATE ROUTES PERMANENTLY PROGRAMMED INTO YOUR DAILY COMMUTE. <u>USE A GPS TO TELL YOU THE BETTER FASTER ROUTE WHEN THERE IS ONE, AND BELIEVE IN IT, TAKE IT. 99% OF THE TIME IT IS THE FASTER OR THE BETTER ROUTE.</u>

The Careful vs. The Careless Driver

To Yield or Not to Yield

Expertise #8

LEAVING AN INTERSTATE AND EXIT ON A CURVING ROAD OUT TO THE RURAL OR CITY STREETS WHERE IT SAYS *YIELD*. I ONLY YIELD WHEN I CAN SEE TRAFFIC THAT I CAN NOT EASILY MERGE WITH. ON THE OTHER HAND, WHEN NO TRAFFIC IS ONCOMING THERE IS NO NEED TO STOP AND YIELD BECAUSE IT IS A YIELD SIGN NOT A STOP OR 'STOP AND YIELD SIGN'. I OBSERVE MANY DRIVERS STOPPING WHEN THEY CAN SEE (AND IT COULD BE THAT THEIR VISION IS POOR-BUT THEN WHY ARE THEY DRIVING IN THE FIRST PLACE?) THE WAY IS CLEAR TO MERGE WITHOUT STOPPING.

THE ABOVE OBSERVATIONS OCCUR IN BROAD DAYLIGHT, NOT ON CLOUDY DAYS OR AT <u>NIGHT.</u>

This next is quoted from a presentation by Jack Melton:

The Careful vs. The Careless Driver

EXITING FROM THE EXPRESSWAY THE EXIT HAS TWO COMPONENTS: DECELERATION LANE - AN ADDED LANE IN WHICH TO SLOW DOWN AND EXIT SAFELY. EXIT RAMP – RAMP LEADING OFF THE EXPRESSWAY OR INTERSTATE. THESE MAY BE LEVEL, SHARPLY CURVED, UPHILL OR DOWNHILL. BE SURE TO ADJUST YOUR SPEED FOR THE RAMP SPEED LIMIT.

There is something intrinsically wrong and outdated: the method of teaching a new driver driving skills by a person who themselves were taught by their mother or father or uncle or aunt. It isn't working. 40,000 deaths in the U.S. annually confirms that. Not to mention the 100,000+ injuries sustained as well, many which hospitalize at great expense and reduce the injured to a status of invalid for the rest of their lives. Have you noticed in the last decade the increasing number of wheelchair icons signifying handicap person/driver? Many of these 'handicappers' are from automobile collisions.

Why Utilize Your Car's Gears?

Expertise #9

Learn to use the vehicle gears in place of always resorting to the brakes of the car. You do realize car manufactures make cars that are automatic with several manual gear settings. This is not done nostalgically, nor to have a reason to put '2ND', '3RD' and 'DRIVE' or 'LOW' 'NORMAL' and 'HIGH' painted on a transmission lever. They're there to be used, <u>especially in city traffic or sluggish interstate traffic where it is not necessary to even use brakes if one is a keenly alert (expert) driver and slows down the vehicle mechanically with its gears.</u> I have twice driven the I 40 <u>in raining conditions from Hermitage to Nashville without once braking, 15 miles one-way and during the infamous Monday through Friday rush hour traffic.</u> Believe it. Drop down one gear, take the strain off the engine, eliminate a lot of unnecessary braking.

The Careful vs. The Careless Driver

ARGUMENTS IN CAR WHILE DRIVING

Expertise # 10

WHEN IT COMES TO ARGUMENTS IN THE CAR, HERE'S TWO WORKABLE REMEDIES: 1) SIT AND GLARE AT EACH OTHER <u>AFTER DRIVING OFF THE HIGHWAY OR INTERSTATE, AND PARKING</u>. JUST SIT THERE AND GLARE. DON'T SAY ANYTHING UNTIL BOTH OF YOU SIMMER DOWN OR YOU START LAUGHING--REALIZING THAT THERE IS A LOT OF *UNKNOWN MATERIAL*, WRONGLY ASSOCIATED, SITTING BEHIND THE ARGUMENT THAT'S OUT OF SIGHT AND NOT LIKELY TO COME TO THE FORE QUICKLY.

SIMILARLY, IF YOU ARE DRIVING WITH SONS OR DAUGHTERS OLD ENOUGH AND LICENSED TO DRIVE, <u>HAVE THEM TAKE OVER AND DRIVE WHILE YOU SIT IN THE BACK IN THEIR SEATS AND PONDER THE MATTER THAT HAS GOT YOU SO RILED UP UNTIL YOU FIND A REASON NOT TO BE SO RILED UP.</u>

<u>2) AND FINALLY, NEVER LEAVE THE HOUSE DURING A SPAT WITH SPOUSE AND DRIVE ANYWHERE. IF YOU ARE A MAN, CALL A FRIEND TO SLEEP IT OFF FOR THE NIGHT OR THE LOCAL PD AND ASK IF YOU CAN SLEEP IT OFF IN A CELL. IF A WOMAN, CALL A</u>

The Careful vs. The Careless Driver

FRIEND OR A SHELTER AND EXPLAIN YOU NEED TO BE AWAY FROM YOUR HUSBAND FOR ONE NIGHT TO COOL OFF. THE POLICE AND THE SHELTER USUALLY WILL BE GLAD TO ASSIST. FAILING THAT, RESORT TO THE REMEDY EARLIER, SIT AND GLARE AT EACH OTHER BUT DON'T SAY A WORD UNTIL BOTH SIMMER DOWN OR START LAUGHING.

QUIZ TIME:

A. You are driving in the low mountains (or high like Denver) during the day and you see ahead a major climb for cars and trucks—medium dense traffic. What do you do?

B. You're driving without having to be at work or some appointment. You drive onto an Interstate or expressway on-ramp to find that there is a *tie-up* and traffic is stalled on all four lanes. (You couldn't see condition of traffic from entrance.)

1) Do you drive on and try to merge into the stuck traffic hoping it will thin out and get moving?

2) Do you try to nimbly back up in the margin and go another route?

3) Do you pull your vehicle off into the far margin and take a snooze until the 1st Responders and PD have removed the obstructing mess?

The Careful vs. The Careless Driver

C. Your vehicle is at a desolate railway crossing in the dead of night. There is a red light that is on facing you for minutes. You are able to see clearly in a straight line 500 to 1000 feet both lateral directions.

1) Do you sit at the light waiting for it to turn green?
2) Do you proceed?
3) Do you sit there and ponder why there is a light at all at the railway crossing?

D. You've just turned your vehicle into an entrance with a mechanical arm that's in the horizontal position. You realize that it is reserved parking for staff only, and you are not staff. There are cars behind you.

1) Do you go through and hope that you will find someone to let you out.
2) Do you sit there in your car waiting for someone to come over to find out why you are sitting there?
3) Do you tell the driver(s) behind you that you made a goof and ask them to back up enough so you can back up and go on to the correct parking facility

E. You are dropping off visiting friends to a hotel and you notice that there are no open lanes except the *Taxi Only* stand. The stand is practically deserted.

1) Do you drop your friends where you have stopped so they can walk the rest of the way.

2) Do you try signaling one of the greeters, on the curb far ahead, that you are stuck.
3) Do you drive deftly and confidently into the *Taxi Only* stand and drop your friends at the hotel main entrance?

What is one of the best ways to avoid 'snail hour' stress?

End of Quiz #1

In <u>*The Careless Driver,*</u> I stated that following too close is a common error on our roadways, especially expressways (Interstates). For many years, the standard was "1 car-length for every 10-mph vehicle speed." Then it was modified to two seconds between the car ahead, judged by counting 'one-one thousand, two one-thousand' from the location of one's vehicle at start of counting [using a post, pole or sign visible that the vehicle ahead just passed] until the counting driver vehicle passes same post, pole or sign.

Two seconds has been stretched to 3 seconds. Why?

It must be that our reflexes our response time as a population of motorists has decreased. No other possibility. Two seconds and the earlier one car-length method <u>were</u> adequate.

So, fellow motorists...predictive, causative driving is a must going forward. Ne cést pas? (Is it not so?)

How is it that a number of females interviewed in *The Careless Driver* drove shift? Their fathers taught them and some of them still drive a manual shift. Are there any benefits to driving in other than the (**D**)rive gear?

Well, we know that most truckers do. We know that race car drivers couldn't function if they didn't. So, what is the big deal about using the gears that are installed in our vehicles by engineers who have been installing them for ages?

The big deal is (as expert drivers know) 1) fuel economy off the bat*, 2) A connected driving experience through better more confident control of one's vehicle, 3) is a must to conquer stress in 'snail hour' conditions. 4) way fewer expensive brake jobs (this any BMW, Mercedes, Lexus, SUV owner etc. is painfully aware of. What is it now, $1300.00 for a <u>front brake repair job</u> at the BMW dealer. WOW!

*Did you know that driving into a wind velocity of as little as 5 mph will hurt the car's fuel economy <u>unless</u> the vehicle is shifted into a slightly higher rev gear? (Not always possible on older cars with only three gears traveling an Interstate at 65 to 75 mph.) For the majority of vehicles (cars, vans, SUVs) this should be intuitive, if it is taught by driving instructors. The slightly lower gear spins faster and with less effort

(just like riding a bicycle with gears) with the result the vehicle labors less and is more fuel efficient. Voila! Takes practice but is attainable.
Expertise, expertise, EXPERTISE. C'mon this is the 21st Century!

During the composing of this new book, I looked into what some of the southern states were doing legislatively to stay current with the now growing trend of requiring more of new drivers to obtain a license to drive. As stated in the earlier book <u>The Careless Driver,</u> the southern states have one-for-one a scaled down and deficient road test required for new applicants compared with states north of the Mason-Dixon line. Georgia for example enacted in 2019 for 2020 statutes the following:

Code Section 40-5-27: "The department shall authorize licensed driver training schools to conduct knowledge tests, **on-the-road driving skills tests,** and other tests required for issuance of a driver's license as provided in this section...**Six hours of private in-car instruction provided by a licensed instructor employed by the licensed driver training school administering such on-the-road driving skills test.**

Looks that in the South the days of "Mom took me out when I was 15 in a grocery store parking lot and let me steer the car," are going to soon be gone for good. And so, will the fatalities that

accrued from such deficient training. Again, as in The Careless Driver: *"The new model eggbeater or washing machine, the latest year's car, all demand some study and learning before they can be competently operated. When people omit it, there are accidents in the kitchen and piles of bleeding wreckage on the highways."*

Let's go over some basic basics that were covered lightly in **The Careless Driver:**

The Careful vs. The Careless Driver

SKIDS

Expertise # 11

During a skid the driver must turn his wheel <u>in the direction of the skid or to do otherwise will increase the sliding/skidding motion of the vehicle.</u> We are, after all, after TRACTION which we have lost in the skid and the better way to do it is <u>take our foot off the accelerator and just steer in the direction of the skid and pump the brakes lightly to slow the vehicle down so we do not start skidding again.</u>

Of course, the <u>best way to handle a skid is to drive expertly, and by that is meant reduce speed downward to a point that is appropriate for the road conditions.</u> And thereby never experience an out-of-control skid scenario.

There was a blizzard in my region a few years back—caught the entire city and suburbs in a complete brace. There was only one snowplow for all roads. (Improved since then, even without any heavy snow.) But the fastest a driver could safely go was 25 mph on the Interstate *in a straight line* such were the icy road conditions and foul visibility. I drove for one hour, then stopped trying to pick up riders (some who called from 45 miles away) And, as I traveled at 20-25 mph headed home I noticed several tractor-trailers

The Careful vs. The Careless Driver

abandoned, sitting off exit embankments unable to even navigate the off ramps.

The Golden Rule Chapter

Expertise # 12

It's time to define a traffic instruction word that we see almost daily if not more than once a day, and that word is **MERGE**. IT MEANS TO BLEND in OR COMBINE SMOOTHLY. See? It doesn't mean to become another person. It has to do only with two objects or vehicles smoothly combining into two vehicles or objects (like airplanes) on the same path. I see immediately as a bonafide example the *Blue Angels* Navy jet elite demonstration squadron with their ultra-close formations and merging and *breaking away* stunts.

Now, in most Interstate on ramps and off ramps there is a dotted line, sometimes quite long, that stretches from the beginning of the off lane to the actual exit and from the entrance to the point where the lane merging coincides with the right-most lane of the Interstate.

Here are some images:

The Careful vs. The Careless Driver

Off ramp

On ramp

Let's take up this one as decidedly the one that gives drivers, especially newly licensed drivers, and I'm afraid also senior aged drivers the most trouble. Why? My idea and from many observations is that the newly licensed driver and the senior aged driver are both concerned about

being let in as they try to inter the Interstate flow. Senior drivers more so because of natural visual impairment due to age only and slower reaction time.

Well, that's why it is a tapered approach. This tapered approach gives the on ramp driver enough time and visibility for the traffic (which shouldn't drive during snail hour in the far right lane) time to smoothly *merge over* to the lane left of their vehicle—provided the oncoming right lane driver has read and applied this book or is by some means already an expert driver.

In the worst possible scenario the on-ramp driver may have to pull into the margin and wait several minutes for the traffic flow to ebb or for at least one driver to slow down enough and signal him/her to get going out off the margin into the flow. Done as a courtesy. Ah yes *courtesy, that boo-hoo'd taboo word in our culture.* A sure sign of weakness or a sign of inconsideration for the 'always late' never on time, never give themselves extra time to get to work or an appointment driving populace who will no doubt take the act of kindness as an affront to them personally and add to it a loud blasting of their vehicle's horn.

♦♦♦

The Careful vs. The Careless Driver

Let's turn some attention on goofy driver practices that are definitely not in the class of expert driving. This is an eye-witness account so I will give it verbatim. Note this occurred in Alabama one of the notorious states for bad drivers and high roadway fatalities:

Karen Banks posted on Spreaker.com
"lol when I was in Alabama I saw a woman with a burger in both hands driving with her elbows!"

So, this next one is my eye-witness and you will soon recall it has been yours: there's a slow moving (slower than the legal speed limit for an Interstate) vehicle moving in the *fast lane or very slow in the far right lane, and the person is talking on their cell-phone!* Typical knuckleheaded driving. Not expert in the least. Now, you say (or to yourself) well, these persons obviously have a *corrupt lifestyle and are out of sync with the rest of humanity.* And, you are right, exactly. But can we and how do we turn this situation around?

Here's the clue: 99% of the time the person has *fixed ideas*. A *fixed idea is one that the person cannot inspect at all.* So, it remains fixed. You can call it to their attention. You can school them on the fact that their actions are dangerous to others, even themselves. You can penalize them with traffic citations and threats of suspending their license. But none of these will alter the fact that they are *operating on fixed ideas*. This is now a scientific fact. A scientific fact that many scholastics and governing bodies have yet to discover, let alone do anything about. But time will tell, and this book will assist.

So, how do we get a person with *fixed ideas* to *unfix?* <u>That's the right question and the right 'problem' to handle, because in most cases the 'other' remedies never **reach the person so as to resolve their fixed ideas.**</u>

In the book <u>The Careless Driver (edition #2) it is mentioned in the chapter on the DUI and Texting Driver that they get cited for what they are doing; they pay the fine, but they also go to a *driving academy.*</u> At the driving academy they get handled on a one-on-one basis by an expert driver. They get treated *individually.* No 'classroom' traffic school <u>talks.</u> The cited driver (now) *'student'* is shown how to drive correctly and responsibly by the instructor. THEN, IT'S THE STUDENT'S TURN TO DO LIKEWISE. Now, the <u>knuckleheadness</u> = fixed idea comes out as protest or alibi or justification because it has to since they won't be passed unless they demonstrate the action they goofed and do it without glossing over it, but really do the driving or driving maneuver <u>for real.</u> The instructor is wise to any ducking out the student may try to pass without sincerity and firmly gets the student to do the action, and as many times as it takes for the student to do it with sincerity.

The Careful vs. The Careless Driver

Now, the scene is set for the real advance. Once the student has voiced his 'fixed idea' and they will, they can now <u>learn.</u> Before this treatment they never even hear what the traffic school lecturer is saying.

The reason, scientifically, this student non-expert driver never gets reached is simple. They are perfunctorily sent to 'traffic school' and along with other offenders can sit in the back (or front, it doesn't matter) and pretend to be taking the class. When in fact all what they are <u>usually</u> there for is to avoid the points and the increased insurance rates that follow a moving violation citation.

Traffic school <u>was</u> the 'old school' approach, it hasn't been winning for a <u>long</u> time. The statistics prove it.

<u>The moral of all this?</u> We have a large portion of our driving population, poorly trained, if at all, in handling powerful and very sophisticated two-ton killing machines (interesting way of looking at it). Driving with sub-standard reflexes to those needed in high-speed close proximity vehicular traffic, and this of course, keeps the nation's auto collision shops busy and in high demand, our hospitals, surgeons, doctors and Emergency Medical Service personnel well supplied with 'victims' of fatal and injurious 'accidents'. Not to mention the tremendous grief and lasting emotional crashes that accompany the

The Careful vs. The Careless Driver

vehicular crashes and the **billions of dollars** spent on *auto insurance.*

Check this statistic: 54% of all collisions occur because of *late braking, or insufficient braking of the vehicle involved.* And this changed perception about our driving skill: It is now a traffic 'rule' to allow "3" seconds between the car ahead and the car that you are driving. It changed many years ago to "2" seconds from the original *one-car length for every 10 mph.* Now its three. And how's this statistic: 1 out of 4 drivers in America, if they continue to drive will experience a collision. This no doubt, if more poor drivers aren't pulled aside or out of the herd and handled as above, we will soon reach 1 out of 3. Pretty grim.

Now, there is a law that I have observed that underlies the foregoing and it is an embracive law:

WHEN a CONDITION or a STATE of AFFAIRS HAS NOT CHANGED in THE DIRECTION DESIRED and MANY ATTEMPTS HAVE BEEN MADE to MAKE it CHANGE in THAT DIRECTION, THEN it CAN BE CONCLUDED ACCURATELY THAT THE FUNDAMENTALS REGARDING THAT CONDITION or STATE HAVE NOT BEEN APPLIED to THAT CONDITION or STATE.

<u>Alertness and driver expertness are not inherent in the human psyche, but they can be trained so that</u>

they are, just as training programs as we grew up gave us our alphabets and our speech recognition and our ability to ride and steer a bicycle; to dress ourselves, to close doors after coming into a house or home and not to open closed doors without knocking first, etc.

It's no use trying to deal with a 2-ton motor vehicle the way we deal with a new oven or a new computer, i.e. *trial and error.*

That's why in the past mothers and fathers would start their progeny learning to drive in a parking lot. But even that was only preparatory or should have been preparatory to training the new permit holder. And by training we mean going out with the new permit holder many times, each time learning a new skill, such as backing up 100 feet (as is required in a Wisconsin road-test) smoothly and in a straight line while looking back as the vehicle covers the 100 foot distance. Practicing changing lanes smoothly with signaling adequately before the change. Merging smoothly onto and off fast-moving (65 mph+) traffic flow Interstates. And so on.

Incidentally, in a recent survey of driver sentiments about other drivers, the top complaint is poor lane changing.

While I was conducting this survey, and I'll share the questions of the survey a little later. While I conducted this survey over a period of several weeks, (100+ surveys) a man I approached said emphatically, "I have a right to drive my car," And, walked away as if insulted. Naturally, I didn't mention to him that this is entirely false, since it is a privilege and will always be one with a heavy responsibility for the pleasure of driving on *public thoroughfares*. If, this man was speaking of his right to own and drive *his car* on *his property* and nowhere else, I concur and would defend that idea to the limit. I believe he wasn't meaning that at all. I'm sure this is not an isolated case.

♦♦♦

I started the survey by stating the following: We need public opinion:
Please help *State* legislators learn what it will take to knock down the annual 1000+ fatalities on TN roadways. (40,000+ deaths each year on U.S. highways.)

Q 1A: How would you rate your feelings about driving Interstates--
  a) Completely at ease and satisfied
  b) Nervous some of the times (if so, circumstances)
  c) Worried most of the time (can you recall circumstances?)

1B: How would you rate your feelings about driving state roads--

a) Worried most of the time (if so, circumstances)
b) Nervous some of the times (specifics) ex: encroaching turners at intersections, running yellow and red lights etc.
c) Completely at ease and satisfied

Q. 2: If new legislation were introduced and passed that requires more extensive road testing for applicants than current testing, coupled with sending convicted *major* moving violators to hands-on <u>driver training</u> instead of 'talk to' traffic school classes, might this alternative have a better result in lowering the number of Tennessee (or fill in State name) roadway fatalities? Y or N (circle one)

Can you estimate which answer was the most chosen?

Can you also come up with the main complaint (negative sentiment) of the survey? (See Appendix for both)

Let's turn our attention to a factor that is pervasive in almost all collisions. Heavy and inappropriate emotions while driving. Here's my example: when in my early years I rode a motorcycle. One day I had a flare up with my girlfriend. On my motorcycle I rode as fast as I could on city streets weaving in and out of traffic going 50 – 55 mph in 35 mph zones. A motorcycle cop put on his siren <u>very loud</u> and proceeded to order me to stop my motorcycle. The officer got off his ride and approached me cautiously with gun drawn and told me to put my hands up, which I did.

After telling the officer that I had a breakup with my girlfriend and was furious he put away his gun and asked for my license and the rest of it as usual.

The officer gave me a stern warning and rode off. He very likely saved my life or at minimum months in a hospital from crash injuries that day.

We have all seen or heard the high-pitched whine of a motor, usually a beefy motorcycle go whizzing by us on an Interstate or past our home that adjoins an Interstate, as one did just before I put these words down. Because this occurrence is the fifth or sixth in as many weeks, I thought to include it. <u>When we lose control of our emotions while driving we can and often will throw out all the rules and especially the expert ones above.</u>

So, the one rule, the one overarching rule is: <u>Keep your cool for as long as you are driving a vehicle, no matter what provocation may occur.</u> Or pull over and let the frustration out in a field or pound some sand or talk with someone and tell them you are *pissed*.

I confronted a man outside my home one night who was brandishing a weapon and screaming to an open window that he was going to kill this girl (soon to be his ex-girlfriend). And he very well might have. But I simply asked him, "What's going on?" He told me and he cooled down. I threw in a little help at that point and said that if she is that unreliable to be with another man, you're better off without her. He put the gun away and left.

Safeguarding Your Chances of Getting Hit

I just finished reading and comparing Michigan's 2016 regulations with 2019 regulations for licensing drivers. If you are in a state that has permissive driving requirements, such as many southern states have had and still to this date have, take matters into your own hands and demand of your state reps and senators that the regulations are made toward the assessment of a new licensee's *demonstrated competence in handling a motor vehicle.* 2016 Michigan regulations even states in their handbook that 30.6 % of all Michigan fatalities are caused by drivers under 25 years of age but the regulation in place in 2016 stated that a driver seeking a driver's license 18 or above from another state need only take a written test. By 2019, one and one-half years after The Careless Driver published, the Michigan state requirements (regulations) now state: "You will have to apply for a temporary instruction permit at a Secretary of State office and successfully pass a driving skills test administered by a third-party testing organization.

We are beginning to smarten up and get the idea. It may have taken more deaths on Michigan roadways to tighten the requirements since 2016 because their fatality total came to 1036 in 2017 vs. 876 in 2014.

The Careful vs. The Careless Driver

Rationale For Handling The DUI and Repeat Offenders - Fixed Ideas

Rationale For Handling the DUI and Texting Driver

Now, let's look at a subject few have a working or complete grasp of. *Fixed ideas* or as the French have it *idée fixé* which is defined: <u>an idea or desire that dominates the mind; an obsession.</u>

<u>What we want to understand it as, is an idea that is not open to inspection by the individual and which poses and enjoins non-survival actions upon them.</u> Such persons as DUI, texting while driving, and repeat traffic offenders will be found to have one or more of these fixed ideas. Now, it was not explained in **The Careless Driver** simply because it would take too long to cover it amply which is why the phenomenon is not fully understood and why governing bodies, driver testing/road testing persons are not set up to detect; but, a qualified instructor on the ball having read this chapter or somehow having come into possession of its information would detect it. So, any traffic violator as cited above will never get the proper education in traffic school talks nor will their fixed idea ever really be revealed so as to expunge it by court room convictions or more and more citations or

even injurious collisions such as a man, Zenon Bialokur, who has 15 DUIs and has killed one person in that 15.

And, we briefly check the news for DUI fatalities (March 2019) and we are appalled at the number of drivers who kill pedestrians and occupants because they are DUI and many times also driving above the speed limit as this driver, at 100 mph. Alondra Selena Marquez, of San Diego, plowed into and killed one of two Lyft passengers as well as incapacitated for life the other occupant. When demanded of her that she take responsibility all she could do was apologize and say that she had no recollection of the crash, and then added: "I need to suffer the consequences."

Another case of 'fixed idea' is Obdulia Sanchez was sentenced in February 2018 to six years and four months in prison after being convicted of gross vehicular manslaughter, DUI and child endangerment. This DUI driver advertised her drinking and driving via Instagram live-streaming and subsequently losing control of her car caused her sister to be ejected from the vehicle and killed.

40,000 or more individuals give up their lives each year in the U.S. because of vehicles colliding with other vehicles, with pedestrians, with motorcyclists and bicycle riders; with trees, abutments, telephone poles--if we count all such deaths, not only the ones at the scene of the crash at the time of the crash. Let's

The Careful vs. The Careless Driver

consider that statistic. Reflect for a moment or two, 40 thousand individuals. Not aliens from outer space sentenced to a violent death here on Earth. 40,000 individuals who had families, friends and associates, living human beings responsible to others whose loss and abrupt disappearance leave an aching vacuum.

Are we so callus, have we devolved into so abysmal a complacency as to completely ignore these facts? Let us instead make real efforts to get control of the situation. Let's make every effort to drastically reduce the number of fatalities by seeing that every driver on our highways and byways is alert 100% of the time they are driving and are well trained to control their vehicle.

CUMULATIVE INSANITY, the actual point between where a person who is sane goes thereafter insane is a very precise point and it's when he begins to stop something (obsessively). At that moment he is insane. Now he is insane on that one subject at first and then he can get another idée fixé and become insane on another subject and you do get cumulative insanity but there is no doubt of his insanity on that one subject.

FIXED IDEAS, 1. the "idée fixé" is the bug in sanity. Whenever an observer himself has fixed ideas he tends to look at them not at the information. Prejudiced people are suffering mainly from an "idée fixé. " A fixed idea is something accepted without personal inspection or agreement. It is the perfect "Authority knows best." It is the "reliable source." A fixed idea is uninspected. It blocks the existence of any contrary observation. Most reactionaries (people resisting all progress or action) are suffering from fixed ideas which they received from "authorities" which no actual experience alters. That British red-coated infantry never took cover was one. It took a score or two of wars and fantastic loss of life to finally break it down. If any single fixed idea destroyed the British Empire, this one is a candidate. *More modernly we have the discovery of Exoplanets i.e. planets that are in a configuration much like our Earth outside our solar system. These observable planets do exist and fly in the teeth of vested interests that say there is only Earth and Heaven.* Some people have a method of handling a downward statistic which is a fixed idea or a cliché they use to handle all down-statistic situations in their lives. These people are so at effect they have some idea sitting there "that handles" a down statistic. "Life is always like that." "I always try my best." "People are mean." "It will get better." "It was worse last year." They know it isn't any use trying to do anything about anything and that it is best just to try to get by and not be noticed-a sure route to suicide. Instead of seeking to prevent or raise a declining stat in life, such people use some fixed idea to explain it. This is a confession of being in apathy. One can always make statistics go up. Hard work, foresight, initiative. That's the truth of it, and it needs no explanations.

The Careful vs. The Careless Driver

Mis-solving problems also leads to vehicular crashes. Take for instance the growing use by truckers in the latter part of the 20th Century, and I'm sure even today but not as widespread, the use of 'uppers' and other pharmaceutical potions to stay awake longer so they could drive longer and further' to 'make more money' by getting their cargo to destinations sooner. Bad solution=no solution.

How can anyone be an expert driver on unnatural stimulants? Can't. Company policy and laws had to be put in place to offset the stupid 'solution' of using uppers, so that truckers have a limit of how many hours they can drive in any 24-hour period. They lose their license and or job if they violate this regulation.

Here's a sample of a state's sane regulation with regards to a new 'rookie' driver (Maryland's MVA New Driver & Coach Practice Guide): "A key part of the Maryland Graduated Licensing System and becoming a safe driver is practice driving 1. You must practice with an experienced, licensed driver **over the age of 21 who has held a license for at least three years.** To complete the required practice hours, you and your coach should start right away. Plan to practice on a wide variety of roads in a wide variety of conditions. When it comes to driving and new drivers, practice does make safer, if not perfect."

If we can train a driver to simply control their vehicle in various weather and road conditions while instilling in them the idea that they don't have to exceed the traffic laws and then *justify doing that,* that driver won't have the compulsion to 'do it again' and most likely not get away with it the second or successive times they violate good sense.

Look, we are not out to get 100% NO FATALITIES. That is ludicrous if even from the fact that rubber tires are sometimes manufactured that have defects in them which cause them to blow out unexpectedly. And how many times has a major auto manufacturer recalled 25, 50, 100,000 or more vehicles because of a reported and documented fault in the operating parts of their cars? In bad weather conditions even the most expert driver can experience a skid especially on newly wet roads by rain or sleet. That's the time when roads give the least traction to vehicles riding over them. But, as an *expert driver* they would be traveling at a much slower speed almost instinctively from the training they received and the fact that they have been groomed to be *highly alert* when driving a vehicle as a given standard.

Conduct an on-line search of airline tragedies. Go ahead do that. (Really-search the Internet for the data.) What did you find? You found as I found that between 50 to 80% of all airline *crashes* were caused by *pilot error. And many of the errors were by* <u>missing or incomplete training of the pilot of emergency situations.</u> I immediately recall Kobe Bryant and his daughter's demise and the undertrained helicopter pilot

The Careful vs. The Careless Driver

who caused the fatal crash. Fascinating isn't it? Highly informative too, yes? Highly illustrative of the need for *training drivers.* Cars are outfitted with many more sophisticated operating 'gadgets' and features than in past years. But not anything close to a jet airliner. Airliners require as many as <u>5000 check overs</u> before hitting the runway each time they start on a flight. Airline pilots require 1,500 hours of flying experience before they are permitted to have a commercial license to pilot a jet airliner! And, in 2010 a co-pilot, called 'a first officer' also requires 1,500 hours training to fly as backup pilot of a jet airliner.

Enough said.

<u>What has worked:</u>

Let's turn our attention to the only *apparent* proven (so far) effective licensing scheme some states have come up with, though the statistics have not been kept by them. The GDL license, Graduated Driver's License.

Here the states, most of which have adopted this system, know that the "training of young or first-time driver licensees" is a vital part of the licensing procedure. Unfortunately, the "training of young or first-time driver licensees" is by adult <u>supervision</u>. **And according to studies once the young driver licensee transitions to 'unsupervised' driving the**

incidence of crashes, though similar to adults **during the supervised period were similar**, it jumps up *dramatically*, and under varying driving conditions.
See:
Crash Risk and Risky Driving Behavior Among Adolescents During Learner and Independent Driving Periods.

(www.ncbi.nlm.nih.gov/pubmed/30006026)

In most cases 'supervised' driving is done by a parent of the youth. This tells us at once that this is an inadequate method of indoctrinating youths *to drive expertly*—though possibly slightly better than no supervision of young drivers. This same study via: The effect of the learner license Graduated Driver Licensing components on teen drivers' crashes - PubMed (nih.gov) shows **Conclusion:** These findings suggest that a learner license duration of at least six-months may be necessary to achieve a significant decline in teen drivers' fatal crash rates. Evidence of the effect of required hours of supervised driving on teen drivers' [across all states] fatal crash rates was mixed.

If we follow The State of Georgia's example as that did become law in 2020, we could do no worse than curbing many collisions by mandating professional instruction of new drivers, young and adult. <u>**The very fact of the instructor holding no kinship or familial relation with the student driver bodes well for a truly objective assessment of the student's ability to control a two-ton vehicle in all road conditions.**</u> **It's also folly to expect that adolescents will uniformly 'listen to' and take to heart instructions from one or the other parent.**

Let's also turn our attention to the nature of the group and individual efforts that are and have been made to halt the unnecessary deaths of individuals and animals from violent collisions of vehicles on our highways and roadways.

In 2016 (and reissued 2019) the NSC (National Safety Council) releases a blueprint calling for a three-step multi-year driver licensing system for teens.

https://www.safetyandhealthmagazine.com/articles/15008-nsc-traffic-foundation-releases-blueprint-to-reduce-teen-driver-crashes.

Recommended requirements include:

- Mandatory in-vehicle technology to track practice hours
- A full ban for one year on transporting passengers and driving at night
- Mandating that parents spend at least 50 hours supervising their teen drivers
- Using license plate decals to identify first-time license holders
- Attending ongoing driver's education courses

Author's Note: *I champion all five recommended requirements especially #4, as mentioned in* **The Careless Driver.** *A similar identification system to #4 is used in Japanese traffic regulations where seniors must display a colorful easy to see decal on their rear window or bumper.*

In 2019 the NSC released their 'Road to Zero' report. This report lays out strategies for ending roadway deaths in the United States by 2050.
Note: The verbiage states 'ending roadway deaths'. This is a sour target because it is unreal to end all deaths by vehicle mishandling merely by the fact that there will be mechanical failures during treacherous road conditions that result in fatalities.

Now, here's what is proposed in these strategies:
Quote from introduction (After years of decline, motor-vehicle related fatalities are on the rise.)

Double down on what works through proven, evidence-based strategies.
Advance lifesaving technology in vehicles and infrastructure.
Prioritize safety by adopting a safe-systems approach and creating a positive safety culture.

"We demand 100 percent safe operations in aviation, marine, pipeline, rail and transit. We should cultivate a corresponding societal demand for safe roads," Deborah A.P, Hersman, president and CEO of NSC, said 19 April press release. "With these three guidelines, everyone can do something to reduce fatalities on the roadway. Getting to zero fatalities is not impossible—it just hasn't been done yet."

Road to Zero Coalition accepting applications for 2019 Safe System Innovation Grants.
https://www.safetyandhealthmagazine.com/articles/17895-road-to-zero-coalition-accepting-applications-for-2019-safe-system-innovation-grants

Then we have 8 Tips to Reduce Road Accidents': www.chevinfleet.com/us/news/8-ways-actively-reduce-accidents

1. Incorporate a Driver Policy

If you have not already done so, developing a driving at work policy that needs to be read and signed for by all of your drivers is the first stage. Your drivers need to be aware of what you are trying to achieve and how – with special attention to their role.

This means providing guidance about:

On-road driving behavior
Inspections that need to be carried out on their vehicles.
Steps to take after the unfortunate event of a collision.
Penalties that are likely to be implemented as a result of poor driving.

2. Get managerial Buy-in

Driving for work is the most dangerous activity many employees undertake and contributes to far more work-related accidental deaths and serious injuries that all other work activities. Lay out some of these facts to explain the extent to which accidents could impact your business operations – and highlight the benefits that could be gained by investing in a road risk management and strategy.
For example, as well as causing human misery, accidents can lead to:

increased insurance costs
vehicle downtime
lost productivity

employee sick leave

missed sales

lost or damaged stock...and more

3. Write a Road Risk Policy

If your employees use vehicles at work, you should make a written road risk policy available to them. This policy should look at your vehicles and drivers and how they are used. It should contain simple and straightforward language to set out objectives for reducing accidents and outline how this will be achieved. The document will serve as the cornerstone of your accident reduction strategy and should be made widely available across your organization.

According to the Bureau of Labor Statistics (BLS) within the U.S Department of Labor, around 40% of motor vehicle accidents are work-related. Released in December 2018, a BLS report – National Census of Fatal Occupational Injuries in 2017 – indicates that driver/sales workers and truck drivers had the largest number of fatal occupational injuries

4. Get accurate information

To reduce your accident rate, you need to know as much as possible about any incidents that have occurred within your fleet.

Careful recording is needed of each accident – not just insurance claim-style details but information on the kind of journey the driver was making, how long they had been driving, whether the vehicle had been recently inspected for safety and more.

5. Benchmark against other fleets

To know whether your accident reduction strategy is working well, it's useful to benchmark yourself against similar companies. Organizations such as **NAFA Fleet Management Association** can help with this.

As part of this process, you will also normally be able to share best practice ideas and discuss which strategies are proving most effective with fleet management peers.

6. Assess drivers' skills

All drivers should be assessed on a regular basis. At the very least, this means checking their driving license and looking at health issues such as eyesight that may affect them on the road. It is also very desirable to assess practical skills through on-road checks of driving behavior by a qualified individual.

Assessments should be especially repeated following accidents and, if there is a question mark over a driver's ability or suitability, they should be prevented from driving for work immediately pending further investigations.

7. Zero tolerance on drink and drugs

You must make it clear to drivers that you expect absolute adherence to the law on driving under the influence of drink and drugs. Many fleets go further and state that drivers should not drive under the influence of any drink or drugs. This policy applies to both prescription and illegal, recreational drugs.

8. Create a road safety culture

Road safety needs to be taken seriously across your organization and considered at every level. For example, there is little point in having a comprehensive accident reduction strategy if employees are placed under pressure by line managers to follow unrealistic schedules or delivery times.

A good idea is to encourage sharing of information from reputable sources, that can help educate and inform on safety measures. For example, *https://www.nhtsa.gov/risky-driving* has a number of tips on driving and road travel safety, whilst https://youth.gov/federal-links/distractiongov can provide customizable policies and other items to display in the workplace.

Author's Note: Many of these caveats are obvious precautionary and preventive measures. But only #6 spotlights driver skills. Because many of these 'truck collisions are involving small trucks even pickups this should top the list at #1.

From Performance.gov

At this URL –

https://obamaadministration.archives.performance.gov/content/reduce-rate-roadway-fatalities-2.html we do have this important and relevant statement: "Distracted driving has emerged as a new threat over the past few years as the rise of portable electronic devices has swiftly expanded. Moreover, as in-vehicle electronic systems become ever more sophisticated and complex, distracted driving could become an even greater threat if it is not addressed in a manner keeping pace with technological advancements."

Author's Note: And, more to the point: "The greatest potential for reducing crashes lies in the difficult task of transforming public and personal attitudes toward roadway safety. Citizens should consider roadway deaths along with the attendant suffering and economic costs as unacceptable rather than inevitable."

And an expert driver both knows the attendant suffering and economic costs are unacceptable but more importantly the expert driver never drives distractedly. *The Golden Rule.*

10 ways to reduce traffic fatalities

1. Every motorist is trying to get somewhere, and many of them aren't sure how to get there. While interstate signage is more or less uniformly good in that it is more or less uniform, rural highway and suburban signage is often quite poor.

Foot-long street signs were fine for city streets where traffic moved at 25 MPH, but 35-45 MPH suburban roads and 55 MPH country roads need bigger signs and more of them: one to announce the next street, one to mark the street at the corner, and one to mark the street beside the traffic light, if there is one. In areas where big trucks are common, extra signage is doubly necessary; trucks have gotten much bigger in the last 20 years and obscure signs to an equally greater degree. This suggestion isn't likely to reduce accidents by much, but it's so cheap it's worth doing anyway.

2. Raise speed limits on safe roads

This would be cheap and effective. By and large, major interstates are broad, well-maintained, smooth-flowing, and well-marked. Raising the speed limit on these roads for cars in daytime and good weather, would encourage motorists to leave dangerous back roads where they know they can drive fast because of limited police patrols. Moving traffic from back roads to major highways was a factor in the decrease of traffic accidents since the 1995 repeal of the national 55 MPH speed limit. Although many states now mandate lower speeds for trucks than for cars, only Texas makes the sensible leap to mandating lower speeds for night driving than for day.

3. Get drunk drivers off the road.

Similarly cheap and similarly effective, discouraging people from driving drunk or otherwise impaired is a proven method of reducing traffic accidents (<u>about half of motor vehicle accidents involve intoxicants</u>). I don't support roadblock checks for impaired drivers—that's a case of surrendering too many liberties for too little gain—but public awareness and messages targeted at bartenders are effective. Just a campaign to ask people not to drive distracted—eating, reading a map, talking on a cell phone, arguing with passengers—would be helpful at little cost. Lower blood-alcohol limits are helping on this front; making more people aware that even a little alcohol impairs their driving.

Author's Note: Again, good sense overall, however the *expert driver* would elect to find alternate methods of travel than driving even if only 'tipsy'. It appears there is a good deal of dancing around the fire instead of pouring gallons of water on it by getting to the heart of collisions and their resultant fatalities, namely driver errors-94%. Let's continue.

4. Implement better roadway lighting

One major factor in motor accidents is poor visibility (half of all motor vehicle accidents are at night, https://benbest.com/lifeext/causes.html even though the great majority of driving is done during the day), especially at intersections, where most accidents occur. If more rural highway intersections were lit, accidents at those intersections would go down. Target intersections with a history of accidents first for best effect and least cost.

5. Create more turn-only lanes

Every car that is stopped in the road to make a turn is an accident waiting to happen. An impaired or inattentive driver colliding with a car preparing for a turn is a major percentage of traffic accidents. Turn-only lanes require little extra roadway but can reduce accidents significantly, especially at intersections with poor visibility for oncoming traffic (around a curve or in a depression).

6. Improve driving conditions

Bad weather always causes a spike in traffic accidents and the cause often gets labeled as "Driving too fast for conditions." State transportation departments could greatly reduce accidents by improving crumbling and pot-holed roads and clearing roads of debris, snow, and ice more efficiently (and closing roads or mandating special low speed limits in especially bad conditions). Intersections where gravel has accumulated are especially dangerous, since cars can easily slide into the intersection when trying to stop.

7. Eliminate stops

Highways are for driving. Any feature that brings all traffic from 70 MPH to 0 MPH is a 10-car pileup waiting to happen as well as a woefully inefficient use of roadway. Moving toll booths to exits is a good start; eliminating them entirely and paying for roads with ordinary taxes is better (you could still make long-haul trucks pull off to pay, as with weigh stations). Creating frontage roads can reduce or eliminate stop lights; so, can funneling traffic from two or three crossroads into a single new overpass. On urban and suburban roads, creating better crosswalks with warning lights that pedestrians can activate can reduce pedestrian traffic accidents significantly.

Author's Note: Can't fault the logic in this #7. Again, all this passes away when we have *expert drivers* on the road *en masse*.

8. Create more divided highways

Any road in which a median separates oncoming lanes of traffic is far safer than ordinary roads. It creates a barrier or buffer that goes a long way toward keeping inattentive and impaired drivers from drifting across the center line and creating a head-on collision, which is nearly always fatal.

They don't have to be four-lane behemoths with clover-leaf junctions; just extra space between lanes with a rumble strip would reduce drifting across lanes and still allow for passing on two-lane rural highways (head-on collisions are almost never the result of passing maneuvers). Although still a new idea, more than a dozen states have begun to use centerline rumble strips, especially Pennsylvania, and report substantial reductions in crossover accidents.

#8 Can't argue with this either—ditto the *expert driver*.

9. Redesign bad intersections

If a crosswalk or lighting doesn't do the trick, a troublesome intersection may simply be designed badly. Paring back vegetation and signage, changing the angle at which the roads meet, or creating a jug handle or overpass are all options that can change the dynamics of traffic at that intersection and save lives.

Just slapping a stoplight in there is not the right way to "fix" it.

10. Redesign bad roads

The US highway system was designed from scratch in the 1950s, and many highways have not changed much since then despite cases of urban sprawl. Traffic engineers have known for decades that left-hand exits create trouble, for example, and should be redesigned whenever there is an opportunity and when traffic snarls and accidents make it urgent. Just designating a highway as a limited-access highway can reduce suburban sprawl around them and avoid the installation of stop lights.

Author's Note: Here's a shared opinion/fact with the author of these 10 methods: "Of course, all of these things cost **money—although some are very cheap—while writing speeding citations actually earns money. It's too bad that writing speeding citations doesn't actually save many lives. (if at all)**

We have, as for citations, the case of 54 year-old Zenon Bialokur arrested 15 times for DUI since 1998, with one fatality to his ignominious discredit. We can see that the act of citing and convicting major traffic rules violators is part of the *'complacency'* we have drifted down into as a nation. The gun doesn't do the killing, the gunslinger/holder of a gun does the killing.

Joel Feldman lost a 20 year-old daughter to a man driving a van who was adjusting his radio when she stepped from curb and was thereafter struck and killed. Joel, who forgave the man and who is an attorney started his own website and

campaign to inform the public at: https://www.enddd.org/about-enddd/distracted-driving-speaker/joel-feldman-esq-ms

He's given more than 700 presentations at businesses, medical, legal and traffic safety conferences and to middle school, high school and college students across the country. Feldman readily admits that even with representing victims of distracted driving crashes he frequently drove distracted until his daughter's death.

We now go to the most distracted type of driver, the criminal and near criminal DUI (or DWI) driver. In **The Careless Driver** it was pointed out that this type of driver cannot be reformed with fines and 'traffic school' lectures. The fundamental reason in all cases of DUI is the loss of respect for themselves and therefore others, which is a characteristic trait of a criminal. The only true and lasting remedy is to have them discharge the mis-emotion (the submerged negative feelings towards themselves and others) they have built up that has warped them into 'another person', a person who doesn't really care, if even for only a few minutes or the time they are driving drunk.

This takes patient understanding and near heroic compassion. What it doesn't take is 'reasonableness' or the idea that this type of person/driver is hopelessly lost and incorrigible, or that massive penalties will have any lasting effect to the good of society. Zenon Bialokur stands as a glaring example, especially since several of his DUIs occurred while driving on a suspended license. We can add Adam Walser and Rudolph Ehrisman to the list of having accumulated 15 DUIs.

For ages, we have known that there are certain individuals around whom accidents and injurious mistakes are made repeatedly. The slang 'jinxed' is a version of this type of personality. In fact, the 'accident prone' term and phenomenon are poorly understood in the main.

Definition: (accident prone) covers exactly, or almost exactly this type of driver: "Having personality characteristics predisposing one to accidents."

Not a medical condition nor a 'chemical imbalance' in their brain. It is an attitude towards existence which the accident prone is barely aware of or not aware of at all and could be classified as a 'fixed idea'; an idea not compatible with and contrary to their lifestyle but is also not available to their inspection. And here we can also include the DUI driver as possessing this characteristic as well as the loss of self-respect. These individuals are also the repeat offenders courts are driven around the bend trying to deal with. And, this is why I recommended in **The Careless Driver** to get these types into a one-on-one situation where they are drilled and drilled on the correct way to drive a motor vehicle and specifically in role-playing the exact scenario for which they violated the traffic law. Drilled not with malice but with that *superior understanding* that here is a person who has sunk below apathy and is operating on stimulus responses to their environment when they drive drunk. No other secular method is going to get them to either cough up the 'hidden and automatic thought process' which makes it O.K. for them to drive distracted, to drive intoxicated, to drive with no possible awareness that they are inexpertly and poorly controlling a killing weapon known as a motor-vehicle.

◆◆◆

Time it Takes to Stop a Motor Vehicle

One of the vital points of 'highly alert awareness' of an expert driver is the time it takes them to stop their vehicle at various speeds. Let's look into this in depth:

With the advent some 20 years since of the modern *full-size* SUV we enter a realm of heavier personal vehicles to the tune of twice the weight as mentioned in **The Careless Driver.** and twice the momentum of a lighter standard automobile. The momentum of a vehicle is defined as 'p' (momentum) = m x v where m = mass and v = velocity (speed in this example). If a vehicle weighs 3700 lbs (the Camaro) and is traveling at 70 mph the 'p' is equal to 3700 X 70 / sec. i.e. every second the vehicles momentum is 259,000 lbs or 130 tons per second. Now, it is clear why it takes 315 linear feet (with good brakes and an alert driver) to slow to a stop a standard automobile. Let's jump into a typical SUV, like the one mentioned in The Careless Driver, a Chevy Avalanche at 7500 lbs. We now see a figure of 525,000 lbs / sec; a whopping 262 tons per second traveling a roadway. How much further than 315 ft. does it require to stop an SUV? A sobering, two football fields length of roadway. Also, an important datum to keep in mind is 54% of all collisions are due to late braking.

All any driver (expert) has to do is find their Vehicle Curb Weight* and plug it into the equation above to find the relative amount of braking force needed and relative time to stop the vehicle they are driving. By the way, an important datum to keep in mind is 54% of all collisions are due to late braking. Bears repeating.

*Weight of vehicle at curb (before passengers and driver get in) and to that their weight has to also be added.

I gave a couple of examples of how a direct hands-on Driving Academy instructor would proceed to deal with the DUI and the Texting Driver; and I want to give another scenario here about the Texting driver remedy. I want to emphasize that the intent of the instructor is to get the student violator to do the action required faithfully, not glibly, and to do it without justification, excuse, protest or alibi--all signs of not registering the meaning of the regulation regarding manually texting while driving. These cases, the DUI and Texting Driver will no doubt be some of the toughest student violators to deal with so it is necessary also to caution and encourage at the same time any instructor to remain positive in his or her control of the student and to not sink into the common reaction of threatening or criticizing the student violator. All in the spirit of making an *expert driver* in the end. These students mandated to personal instruction at their expense already have paid fines and possibly attorney fees, so firmness but with superior understanding is a necessity.

<u>Driving Academy Instructor Handling Texting Driver Senario:</u>

<u>Have the student in their car. The instructor texts them while driving using a picture of their boyfriend (girlfriend) as it applies and get them to not respond but keep driving or pull off the roadway and stop.</u> Drill that until that particular skill is indoctrinated properly to a result. I would also counsel Driving Academies who take on this 'novel' student, to keep a record of their license and checkup now and then to see if they have in fact reformed and are driving at a much more expert (and safe) level. A quality assurance statistic definitely but more importantly a guide for the Academy owner / instructor to use to adjust training for improved results going forward. This privilege to keep track of 'novel' students should be extended by courts of jurisdiction or by legislation as it is ultimately in their interests to so provision.

The Careful vs. The Careless Driver

Lastly, only the experts in a field or endeavor can truly be or attain security and longevity. Whoever heard of a mediocre dancer, actor, architect, attorney, sculptor living well and surviving well?

They don't. And the mediocre driver won't survive well either. Why not master the activity, driving, an activity the bulk of working and living persons do more than any other activity bar sleeping and eating. For that matter why not master living while we are at it, one action, one activity, one field at a time? Train to attain mastering of driving and lower the possibility to practically nil of dying painfully in a collision with other vehicles or killing a pedestrian or occupants of other vehicles.

Sound good?

The Careful vs. The Careless Driver

The Careless Driver
2nd Edition

(aka The Distracted and Undertrained Driver)
By
Charles Van Heyden
With updated statistics and chapter on
The DUI Driver.

The Careful vs. The Careless Driver

Velvet Gloves Publishing
Nashville, Tenn

© 2017 Velvet Gloves Library
2nd Edition © 2018-2020

ALL RIGHTS RESERVED

Printed in The United States

Contents

Author Forward	**5**
Preface	**7**
Interviews with Driver Training School Instructors	13
National Highway Traffic Safety Admin. Data	23
Initial Interviews with Drivers	27
Interview, Lee with data from Japanese friends	39
Interviews with Texas and Central India driver	45
Interviews-Amy (AL), Tim (NC), & Levi (OH)	53
Interview with Rajat from India and Ryan (Tenn)	61
Interview-John (KS) Thomas (TX) Elaine, Chris/Rajiv	65
Interview with Trevor (Buffalo, NY)	77
Interview with Geeta and Glen	83
Interview with Carlos from the Philippines	95
Interview-Allison (N.J.) & Marisa (Chicago	101
Interview with Patrick from Rwanda	111
The DUI Driver & The Texting Driver (2nd Edition)	121
Author's summation & conclusions plus additional statistics	127
Legislative Acts Introduced	135
Appendix	145
Acknowledgements	147
About The Author	149

The Careless Driver

AUTHOR FORWARD
(From back cover)

The Careless Driver *is written from extensive professional experience as a chauffeur and driver in all types of environmental conditions, traffic flows, and road conditions. My observations and conclusions and recommendations are added to live interviews with drivers in the book detailing the types of errors and misinstructions that many drivers upon our interstates and roadways have become accustomed to demonstrating. These details are the 26 candid interviews with drivers from foreign countries, and other states than and Tennessee, with what those states and countries require to license drivers.*

I have great hopes that the information in this book and the non-accusative manner in which it is delivered will find a large audience with parents, driver training school owners and instructors, traffic court judges, and DMVs, as well as the general driving population of America. (Possibly not with auto insurance companies.) More and better driver training should ensue with noticeable reduction of fatalities, especially among our youth.

PREFACE

WE AS A COUNTRY HAVE SUNK INTO A COMPLACENCY ABOUT VEHICLE DEATH AND HOMICIDE ON OUR ROADWAYS, WHILE MANY STATES REQUIRE LITTLE IN THE WAY OF DRIVING SKILLS TO OBTAIN A DRIVER'S LICENSE. Can anything be done about the yearly 35,000 plus deaths of humans caused by inattentive and unskilled drivers? Few, if any of the motor vehicle drivers that irritate, annoy and scare you do it with malice. What I've observed is that they <u>drive inexpertly</u>.

It is unlikely that anyone has taken the time and effort to observe, analyze *directly and record* the driving habits and practices *from* drivers to the extent this work does. This may be the first. Hopefully the data about them will assist Driver Training Schools, The State Departments of Public Health (DMVs), parents of teenagers, traffic courts, and give drivers across America who read this book an opportunity to see where we have erred in our insufficient *driver training*, and where we can lower the stress substantially with and in the rush hour Interstate or highway traffic conditions due to the presence of under-educated, <u>under-trained drivers.</u> Let us now define what a Careless Driver is.

The Careless Driver

<u>DEFINITION-Careless Driver:</u> Distracted driver or an impaired driver, this leads to a remedy more suitable and more quickly. This includes a driver who is not one hundred percent present when driving a vehicle. <u>Note:</u> This last sentence, in body, is at <u>the very end of lengthy descriptions in state codes about the 'negligent' and 'careless' driver with some states omitting it entirely.</u>

<u>Definition-Careful Driver:</u> A driver who by their expertise alone can be a calming influence to other motorists, who are driving distractedly. This includes slowing down many hundreds of feet in advance of a collision or bad merging section of highway. It includes reporting motorists who come up suddenly and cut into another drivers lane without signaling or drive at top speed right behind another car so as to bully them out of their path or similar reckless/dangerous driving.

For myself, I have chauffeured thousands of individuals. And, while doing so have had the opportunity to drive in all types of weather, roads and traffic conditions, seeing all types of driver *driving* weaknesses and errors. Having great familiarity with driving in cities, rural towns and on Interstates and seeing the enormous amount of poor driving, daily, I decided to launch a grass-roots survey into driver *driving habits and practices,* as well as their training or lack of it, and see if there was anything to learn. I decided to interview at random a number of my passengers/riders, several from other countries and states, and compile their candid stories of how and when they first learned to drive, and any further driver training that they may have experienced. Let's see whether or not there <u>is something that can be done to get driving back to a pleasure again.</u>

The following interviews were done throughout the Spring and Summer of 2017 with passengers in my chauffeured vehicle. They represent a factual cross-section of types of drivers, not only from Tennessee but other states and other parts of the world. The following 26 plus interviews with drivers and 2 interviews with major city owner/instructors of Driver Training Schools should prove eye-opening, and in many cases very surprising. Of the 28 interviews, several are of naturalized citizens living here in the U.S., from India, Kazakhstan, the Philippines, Nepal and Japan. We will see as we read through that these countries see driver training in a much different light, and why. Highway deaths had been steadily dropping to approximately 35,000 compared with earlier totals of 50,000 plus. But 2016 has seen a substantial increase, now the deadliest year in nearly a decade. (Read online article: fortune.com/2017/02/15/traffic-deadliest-year) <u>Note: This second book you are</u>

reading was published before the first book by two years.

Statistics for roadway fatalities 2017 will not be available until December 2018! The truly sad part of these statistics is *too* many gifted artists have been taken from us by automobile crashes: Patti Santos (age 40) of *It's A Beautiful Day*, Jimmie Spheeris (Motorcycle-age 34), Duane Allman (age 24), Steve Allen, noted comic and TV host. But why settle for even 35,000 deaths or permit thousands of deaths and a million times that amount in damaged bodies, hospitalized bodies and ruined property? Why? That is what this work also seeks to spotlight, but with a positive answer. It should be known that the Graduated Driver License (GDL) program of many states has been the only effective program, up to 30% reduction in fatalities, but again why stop there with only *beginner drivers?* **What if we as a nation expensed a small fraction per capita (per driver) of the billions spent yearly for auto insurance, but on professional driver training?**

The author's questions, responses and comments are underlined for easy recognition, but the answers, though verbatim from the recordings, are not in quotations for simpler assimilation and conveyance. (Meaning transcribing, editing, proofreading time, and effort.) The recorded interviews are in relatively sequential date order. Statements/words in parentheses ( ) are to the reader. First names only are used. Some, only a few, had difficulty in recalling data that was asked for in the interview, and this is sometimes footnoted or noted directly in parentheses also. I did try to not repeat the same questions, mainly since in most cases there would not be enough time for the passenger to answer a battery of questions. Also, to get at a variety of scenarios and driving practices polled. And sometimes there will be an "End." at the end of an interview, when it is not completely apparent that the interview is finished.

As a footnote: the driver errors on surface streets observed by myself when driving more than thirty thousand miles a year, combined with the errors and misinstructions found in the interviews that follow are intensified where they are observed on Interstates, where the flow of cars and trucks/buses is substantially faster requiring more skill and *alertness* than on city or rural roadways.

Usually, there are more miles of non-Interstate roadways than Interstate roadways in any given state. And the Interstates are mostly used by motorists during the day hours and at *rush hour.* So, it is telling that for Tennessee and most states (2016 data), there are more deaths per road mile on Interstates than on other major and minor *arteries,* as they are referred to

The Careless Driver

by the National Center for Statistics & Analysis (National Highway Traffic Safety Administration – NHTSA)

The remedies proposed in later chapters by no means constitute the sole resolution to significantly lowering the incidence of deaths and injuries on our roadways occasioned by unalert, distracted, impaired and under-trained drivers. As a Nashville Councilman who has read this book stated: "[Our city] is working on reducing traffic fatalities by lowering speed limits and evaluating our most dangerous intersections. This looks like an additional part of the solution."

The Careless Driver
(The Under-trained Driver)

Pitner Driving School (Memphis, TN) provides six hours of practical driving instruction of the thirty hours in the course that it delivers. Their main client is the parents of youths about to get a car, ages 16, 17, 18. They are, by the owner Mr. Pitner's perception, of Pitner Driving School, that his is the top of several driving/traffic schools in Memphis, Tennessee. Here I want to again make a distinction between traffic schools (that instruct about the rules of the road and safe driving practices) and *driving schools* that give the hands-on training to new adult and young drivers so that they are better equipped to handle the fast-paced Interstate driving situations and dangers.

Note: This interview, was not conducted with a recording as were all the driver / rider interviews done first-hand and recorded. Notes were taken as the questions posed were answered.

Further, Mr. Pitner went on to say that his instructors take their students out onto the Interstate and educate them in how to merge correctly with the faster moving traffic, and this done repetitively until the student can do it confidently. "We won't take the student out when it is raining or snowing," stated Mr. Pitner but we plan for doing that practical instruction

The Careless Driver

on another schedule if the weather doesn't permit us to deliver the hands-on training due to inclement weather conditions. Although the driving school's curriculum is not posted on the Internet, each day the student goes out with the instructor, notes are taken and brought back to be typed up by the school's secretary and presented to the parents of the student after the thirty-hour training.

<u>Phil</u>:
who is an instructor for Brentwood Driver Training Program (Brentwood – near Nashville, TN): "[We're] the only completely dual control, we have steering wheels, we have brake pedals, we have gas pedals. Other schools only have brake pedals. [Those that] take our class get four hours behind the wheel instruction, or six hours more, two of which are behind simulators. We're open to persons purchasing lessons outside of that. So, I've had people get as many as twelve two-hour lessons. Or as few as one. It's mainly adults. The ones that buy that many is because they move here maybe from out of country and don't have the support structure to practice as much. With the teenage students, typically their parents drive with them more.

We take them (students) out anywhere from 9:00 AM to 7:00 PM, Monday through Saturday. I've had students who have driven in rainstorms.

The Careless Driver

<u>Do you repeatedly take (students) out to the Interstate to teach them to merge with traffic properly?</u> I do as much as I can. I tell them to wait until the dotted line portion (ends and not [cross] the solid line. And tell them to not rush through it. Use their signal, look for an opening before you go. Try to get your speed up, before you go. Try to get your speed up to the speed of traffic before you get over. I try to do it multiple times. Sometimes I'm limited by traffic. If I'm in rush hour traffic and it's a two-hour lesson I may be able to merge on maybe once, twice at the most. Most of us [our instructors] try to get our students on the Interstate at least once during a lesson. You may not get the full opportunity to merge like more than once but most of us try to take them on the Interstate at least one time.

*Note: Phil states, "Try" in answering but it is not the optimum level of skill needed. Drivers of Interstates <u>must</u> merge smoothly or slow-downs and collisions result.

<u>What about following too closely?</u> We teach them the two-second rule. Because it increases the distance based on speed. Something we always teach in our driving school, following safely. Changing lanes from the slower to the faster lanes as you go left. We teach them not to break while shifting lanes—from left

lanes to right hand lanes. That sometimes you must speed up. But you want to base what you're doing on the traffic. If the cars next to you are going over your speed, you know faster, you want to accelerate into that lane.

How do you teach them to know that, to be aware of that? You can gauge how fast drivers are going and have their pedal usage reflect what they're seeing in their mirrors. How successful do you think you are with your students? I'd like to be more successful but most of the time if they have two lessons with me, *then I'll see a noticeable difference in their driving.* (That's the standard?)

Have you seen anybody stopping on the Interstate merge lane with no Yield sign? I haven't had students do that because I have pedals on my car, but I've noticed-obviously, I won't let them do that. I've seen other drivers do that while with my students. It's a great learning opportunity to point it out later.

Tell me about looking ahead. We teach them to keep their eyes elevated where the two lines on the side of the road come together in the distance to a focal point, and their hand eye coordination helps them to stay between the lines. I tell my students it's a similar (inaudible word) like when you throw a baseball to

The Careless Driver

someone you don't look at the ground in front of you. You look at them and your body just gets it there. What about when they get behind the Escalades and the Avalanches (wide SUVs)? Tell them to create more distance, so they can keep their eyes off without getting so close to the car in front of them. You must teach them how to pay attention to the cars in front of them without focusing too much on just that car. So, see the brake lights, see what's happening but while keeping your eyes elevated.

Here's the million-dollar question-do you teach any of your students that the gears are not just for accelerating but they are also for decelerating? Not really. It doesn't come up that often. I mainly just teach them to brake whenever they are going down a hill, something like that[1]. I mainly teach my students to use the brake but that's primarily so that the drivers behind us will know we are braking and slowing down, because with a student driver car they are much more likely to hit their brake too hard or just *brake at the wrong time.* (???) I try to get the drivers behind us alerted so that we are slowing down.

Have you taken any students out in a parking lot to show them how to handle a skid? It comes up in the

---

[1] And this is from where comes the bad practice of braking going down a hill when not necessary. Alert drivers don't need a brake light to see a car is slowing.

The Careless Driver

lesson all the time. I don't typically take them into a parking lot to show them that, but I'll take them into a neighborhood and drive around and show them what happens if they accelerate too hard or brake too hard. It comes up at least one time, every time it rains.

What about turns on the Interstate—do they really know how to take the turn correctly, because I see a lot of drivers braking into the turns instead of braking before the turn. Yeah, I teach them where to brake, stuff like that. And where to accelerate.

One more thing—emergency vehicles, actually I've asked many people, for inclusion in this book, and I have noticed invariably, when there is a collision, even if it on the other side of the Interstate [drivers] slowing down. Yeah (Phil chuckles),
It's a rubberneck*. What are you trying to do, cause another accident and slow traffic down even more? Yeah, I tell my students if it's not on your side of the Interstate there really is no reason to overreact to it. Read about it in the news later.
*rub·ber·neck [ˈrəbərˌnek]
Verb: turn one's head to stare at something in a foolish manner: a passerby rubbernecking at the accident scene. "A passerby rubbernecking at the accident scene." Oxford Dictionaries © Oxford University Press.

The Careless Driver

Here is an example of the effort being made in local areas to improve driving habits: DEFENSIVE DRIVING CLASS: On Saturday December 9, from 9 a.m. to 3 p.m. there will be a New York State approved Defensive Driving Class. Save 10% on your base auto insurance for the next three years & receive up to 4 points off your driving record according to New York State Department of Motor Vehicle guidelines. The class will be held at First Baptist Church, 45 Washington Street, Saratoga Springs. Fee $35. Bring a friend $30 each. A portion of the fee will be donated to First Baptist Church. Registration is required and can be made by calling Ray Frankoski at 518-286-3788.

As we can see the incentives are skewed towards saving $ on insurance and vacating or nullifying points against one's driver record. Ideally, persons attending should be attending to acquire skills resulting in improvement as *drivers*. Only hands-on *practical instruction* behind the wheel of a vehicle is going to provide that kind of improvement.

These are a few of the many driving faults seen on Nashville Interstate and surface streets and elsewhere:

#1 Following too closely the vehicle immediately in front.

#2 Braking instead of gearing down to slow the vehicle (in conjunction mainly with #1.)

#3 A. Stopping on an Interstate on-ramp merge lane with no Yield sign,

3 B. Also merging slowly onto an Interstate highway more slowly than the traffic traveling in the immediate left lane.

#4 Changing lanes abruptly in heavy traffic after only one or two flashes of directional signal.

#5 Slowing down for an Emergency Vehicle with emergency lights flashing when an open lane, two lanes away is available safely.

#6 Slowing down to view an accident on the Interstate* instead of smoothly and with enough notice, changing lanes and getting away from the injury area. (Requires training in looking five to 10 cars ahead) *Including collisions and Emergency vehicles *on the other side of the Interstate middle barrier.*

#7 Left hand turners that turn too early into the oncoming traffic not allowing for the cars ahead that turned to clear the intersection, but blindly following another vehicle ahead and into the path of oncoming vehicles. In other words, misjudging the approaching vehicles in the opposite direction.

#8 A vehicle comes to STOP ON RED, the driver stops and remains there thinking he must stop for red light *and remain there,* even though he is turning right. Also, likewise, on the corner of Bowling Avenue and

The Careless Driver

West End, we have a NO TURN ON <u>FLASHING</u> RED LIGHT, but many times it'll be a red light <u>not flashing</u> and the driver or drivers will be stacked behind each other waiting for who knows what.

#9 Changing lanes on Interstate from slower (right) to faster (left) at speed slower than traffic in left lane.

#10 Looking at only car in front on Interstate (during rush hour especially) instead of looking five to 10 cars ahead, that would alert driver to slow -downs in traffic coming up (most often at Interstate interchanges).

#11 Nashville drivers: unnecessary waiting at red light with four lanes of traffic (2 each) in each direction and *there is no traffic approaching in the nearest lane.*

#12 Again, Nashville drivers, obvious, <u>blatant</u> common error is merging on to fast moving Interstate they will try to maintain speed and not accelerate to merge or even will slow down with several vehicles behind them trying to get on to the Interstate, causing a blockage and potentially a rear-end collision.

#13. (Added after witnessing multiple examples) I've seen drivers close to a vehicle change lanes before signaling or immediately after signaling on the Interstate or surface streets. I've gotten this as a complaint from many passengers not just the passengers I interviewed.

#14. Unawareness by a majority of drivers that lower gears give driver better control of vehicle and a more connected driving experience?

The Careless Driver

<u>Note:</u> All modern SUV's have sequential gear shifting capability and should be used with the training of how and when to shift *up*. (To a higher rpm gear—which slows the vehicle mechanically, internally instead of burning/wearing out the car's brakes and necessitating excessive braking when not needed.)

GENERAL DATA ABOUT DEATH RATES-WORLD-WIDE

The Careless Driver

The Careless Driver

<From zholpolice.kz [then to */pdd>* Excerpt from Russian police. (Be aware this site is sometimes down for routine maintenance and / or problems.)
10.1. The driver must drive the vehicle at a speed not exceeding the specified limit, taking into account traffic volume, characteristics and condition of the vehicle and its cargo, road and weather conditions, in particular the visibility of the direction of travel. <u>Speed should provide the driver increased control over movement of the vehicle to fulfill the requirements of the Rules.</u> (My underline)

National Highway Traffic Safety Admin. Data

The U.S. has seen a 31% reduction in its motor vehicle death rate per capita over the past 13 years. But compared with 19 other wealthy countries, which have declined an average of 56% during the same period, the U.S. has the slowest decrease. Road death rates in countries such as Spain and Denmark have dropped 75.1% and 63.5%, respectively.

If the United States had reduced its death rate to the average of other countries, 18,000 more lives would have been saved, according to the CDC report. cnn.com/2016/07/07/health/us-highest-crash-death-rate.

The Careless Driver

The title of this book is **The Careless Driver**. However, it is sub-titled *The Under-trained Driver*. And, in this we discover a resolution much easier to accomplish than any other put forward to date. As a renowned educator observed: **"The new model eggbeater or washing machine, the latest year's car, all demand some study and learning before they can be competently operated. When people omit it, there are accidents in the kitchen and piles of bleeding wreckage on the highways."** Just *how much learning* is needed with regards to motor vehicles should become by end of this work, strikingly apparent.

The Careless Driver

INITIAL INTERVIEWS

The Careless Driver

The Careless Driver

Joe on 18th May. He learned from his grandfather at age 14, Dixon TN. His mother also instructed him, but she was always nervous in the vehicle. Had no formal training, school or driving school. Talked about speed limits, driving in the rain, driving on the Interstate. Grandfather never took him on the Interstate, only the back roads around the farm. Neither did his father or mother. Father who was paying the insurance, wanted Joe to drive at 5 mph under the speed limit, whereas grandfather said it is OK to drive 5 mph over speed limit. Grandfather taught him at night avoid the glare of oncoming headlights, how to slow down ahead of a curve. Other than that, Joe had very little training about driving on highways and especially super-highways. Approximate age is 38, he stated he got his license age 16 and that was 22 years ago. First interview for the book *The Careless Driver*.

CJ (African American guy) and I are headed to Walgreens on 5th Ave, Nashville: <u>Who taught you how to drive first?</u> CJ: It was probably split between my parents. Both my mom and my dad. I live out in the country, so if we...in an empty parking lot, or driving through the country, they let me drive where it was uncrowded, unpopulated, so it would be safe. <u>What did they teach you basically in the beginning?</u> Honestly in the beginning, cause it's an adjustment when you first get behind the wheel, on how to actually steer the vehicle and stay on the right side of the rode. How touchy are the brakes and gas. Be prepared to look at your side-view mirrors. <u>How many hours of education from dad and mom you had?</u> Probably over 10 plus hours. <u>Then you got a permit and drove yourself?</u> Then I had to take a class in high school, your sophomore year you take Driver's Ed. too. <u>What did that consist of?</u> That consisted of school, like academic learning from a book, and you got to drive around in a car with your teacher too. Certain days that you went out. Also, you got and a driver's permit allowing that you could drive with anyone over the age of 23. Logging so many hours before you could get your permit. I got my permit in Illinois valley, Cook County. <u>I want to make sure that for the book, when I write it up I'm going to have the people *who are educated here*, *the people who are educated in another state, and other countries*. I'm going to break it down into three different areas.</u> Good. <u>Because I have interviewed people from Kazakhstan and India.</u> O.K. <u>CJ, when you went out with your instructor you had dual controls, right, what was the main thing he tried to stress with you?</u>

The Careless Driver

I was really bad when I first was learning to drive. I was trying to be extra cautious.

Honestly, the main thing I remember were the days we went on the highway (Interstate 80). I was really bad when I first was learning to drive. I was trying to be extra cautious. So, when I was merging onto to the highway I would be coasting there, and my speed wouldn't be the right speed to fall in with the other cars. So, he was always stressing that I need to accelerate when I was coming off the ramp and decelerate when coming onto regular roads. That was the biggest thing I took away from that." <u>Was that the Interstate or major highway?</u> Interstate, yeah. <u>I-80, I know it well.</u> Good, <u>Now, did he take you out in the rain?</u> Did he take us out in the rain? Um...I don't know if it ever rained while I was...<u>Well, then they would...</u> That would just be then situational. I know that when I was with my parents, I had driven in the rain before. <u>Oh, really? They were instructing you?</u> Yeah, obviously they were giving me pointers and saying like, don't adjust your turns or anything for the rain, cause if you are going too fast, you'll slide. Just little things—it's more common sense when you think about it now, but then it was, just make sure you stay calm (garbled few words). <u>Now, on dry pavement did they tell you</u>

The Careless Driver

<u>how to take turns at 60 mph speed limit type highway—you want to go up on a nice little curve...gradually like that (author indicates curve with hands)?</u> It was more just about *now you won't have to check the [steering] wheel over to the side or anything.* I think my dad would always tell me, my dad would say: "When you are driving look at a point ahead of you." "Keep the nose of your car on that point where you are looking. Always have your eyes ahead of you so that way wherever your eyes go your hands will turn with it too." "When you are going on a gradual turn and you have your eyes a little bit in front of you, you'll gradually turn with it instead of looking all the way to the right and just turning your wheel back to the right." <u>Right, good advice. Now, what about rush hour traffic—did your father or instructor ever take you out in *rush-hour* traffic in Illinois?</u> I was from a small town, so I never had rush-hour traffic. So, no, I did not get to experience that, until I went to college out near to Chicago. <u>So, you went to Chicago, big city, lots of traffic: then how did you learn, who taught you there?</u> From there-- It was more or less about me learning by himself. I kinda took things that my parents taught me, while driving around my town. Just applied it to a bigger scale, honestly. The biggest thing with rush hour traffic is staying calm. If—it's like when I was going up there my parents would give me tips before I went. But, I was by myself when I first went into traffic and everything. They said, "If you are

The Careless Driver

overly passive you will get into a wreck too." "You have to hold your own at some point." (Laughing) You know what I mean, don't be overly aggressive, but also don't be overly passive either. <u>Okay, Okay: Did any of your instructors, mother, father, teachers in high school, take you out and try and get you into situation where the car would skid—so you could learn how to handle a skid?</u> Um…yes. My dad, my instructor in school did not. My dad, a driver for UPS. He drives big six axle rigs like that. <u>Right, the long trailer.</u> On Sunday he would pretty much have to drive 35 minutes, so I was driving in the winter too. There were times when there was snow. So, I was in situations where the car could have slid but it didn't. He told me what to expect when the car does start to slide. <u>And, since that time you never have had an actual skid?</u> Oh, yeah, no I've had skids before. <u>How did you handle it?</u> Well, I just went back to what my dad had told me. When your car fishtails turn the wheel the opposite way and it will straighten it back out. (Not the correct method.) <u>If the back end comes out, you want to turn your wheel to the way the tail is going.</u> (That is the correct method.) <u>So, this is to the left, so you turn the wheel to the left.</u> To the left. Yeah. (Laughing) First time I kept spinning in a circle. <u>(Dropped off CJ at convenience store.)</u>

<u>All right it's the 27th of May we are riding with Chandler, to his restaurant work. He's telling me his</u>

33

mom let him drive around in a parking lot-what age were you? (Stated that he first learned about cars and driving from his mom who with him in her lap let him steer in a parking lot. Age 10. Guess mom wanted you to get going quick, huh? That's good. Then, what did she have you do? I wouldn't be in the driver's seat, I was trying to control the steering. (Inaudible) My sister would let me drive around the neighborhood before I even had my permit. So that's how I got started. And, then did you get any formal instruction in High School? No, I didn't take any driver's ed. (Started driving on his own at age 15 down one street to grocery store.) Did you have an uncle or male figure help you out? No, never had anyone. Okay then, when did you start driving on your own? When I got my permit at 15, I would run errands for my mom like—where we lived at the time we had a grocery store right down the road, so she trusted me not to be able to drive without my permit (Meaning, her in the car.) just down one street. Then once I got my license, I just started driving wherever I wanted to go. Okay, okay, very good-and, how would you rate yourself on a scale of 1-10 as a driver here in Nashville? I would say about an "8". Only because I do speed. I'm really bad at speeding sometimes, especially on the Interstate normal rate. Have you been in a car that skidded on wet pavement? No. How far ahead, when you are on the Interstate, are your eyes focused? Pretty far ahead. Of course, I like to see

The Careless Driver

the car in front of me. But sometimes I can see what I am dealing with if there is no one way ahead of me. Also, it depends on what time of day. <u>How are you at merging into rush-hour traffic?</u> I'm great. I know a lot of people (drivers) don't like it, but I you know I'm one of those drivers that if I know that I have to make a left turn or a right turn I *stay* in the left or right lane. I'm not one of those [drivers] who waits to get over to the right at the last minute. <u>Tell me about Yield Signs.</u> I slow down...I honestly stop at Yield Signs, just because you never know, but in neighborhoods if it's a yield sign I definitely do slow down. <u>O.K. how about stop signs where you can see clearly left and right for two hundred yards?</u> Of course, I stop at a stop sign, do you mean a 4-Way? <u>Let me asks that question again: You're coming to a stop, but you can see there is no traffic visible left or right and no traffic coming your direction?</u> Oh, I see, I still stop. <u>Do you teach anybody else how to drive?</u> Yeah, my stepsister, and she has her own car now, and that's how she got started. <u>And how is she doing?</u> She hasn't wrecked yet...so. I live on my own so haven't seen her lately. <u>Okay, let me pause this right here.</u> (To locate his drop off place.) <u>So, you think speeding is one of the situations with drivers here, and they are rude. Interesting. And, when you say speeding, what does that consist of? That's a relative term unless we have something to compare it with.</u> Speed limit here is 75 mph, but if I were driving, I would probably be going

The Careless Driver

60. You have the internal flow of traffic and it is easier (inaudible). <u>Are you aware of any laws or covenants amongst drivers that it is a good idea to drive at the same speed as the flow of traffic?</u> I'm not too sure, but I [drive] not too much faster because that would mean (inaudible). <u>Have you taken any long trips yourself in your vehicle?</u> No. <u>Okay let's finish it here.</u>

(Caroline visiting Nashville from Atlanta, GA off-recorder: says her father taught her the basics of driving a car. Then she had an 8-hour driver's ed. class in high school. Took her out, told her about turn signals, 3-point turns. No, or very little training on Interstate driving.)

(Elizabeth delivered her to Vanderbilt U. no formal training driving a car. Her friend let Elizabeth use her car in a parking lot. Got her permit in Nashville. No training or instruction from father or mother. No professional instruction.) <u>Just a couple of penetrating questions about your driving habits. How would you rate yourself on a scale of 1-10, on merging onto Interstate rush-hour traffic?</u> Well, I haven't been in an accident... (unintelligible). <u>Describe how you would do it getting onto Interstate traffic Monday morning (rush hour)?</u> I don't know. I don't know what you are asking me. <u>Getting onto the Interstate-do you do that at all?</u> Uh, uh. <u>Okay. Tell me what you are looking for and how you operate the vehicle that gets you onto</u>

The Careless Driver

the Interstate. I don't know what you mean, like? I don't know. Pretend that you are driving this car onto the Interstate right now. Uh, uh. In rush-hour traffic. How would you tell me to drive? (Considerable hesitation before eventual answer.) Come on! (Forced laugh.) I don't know what you mean, like.... Let's say you're driving this car and not me, okay? And I'm going to get on the Interstate. Well, I would get into the right lane... Go down the ramp, I don't know. ____ cars. Hm, hmm, what about the speed of the vehicle? Progressively faster as I'm going down the ramp. Do you wait for cars on your left side to go past you? While I'm on the Interstate? While I'm on the ramp? (Said quizzically) On the ramp. Do you wait for cars on your left to go past you? Yes. O.K. Do you slow down to let them go ahead of you? Not if I'm going on the Interstate. Hm, hmm. Have you ever found a situation where a tractor-trailer was on your left and you slowed down or came to a stop? Never a stop...but have to slow down. What was thought process that made you slow down and not speed up ahead of the tractor-trailer? (Typically, tractor-trailers stay out of the right-hand lane, and travel slower than most of the traffic.) It was way bigger than my car. (Laughing) Got it. Can you recall a time when that happened recently? (No.) But it did happen? Sure. O.K. Let's turn this off. End.

The Careless Driver

The Careless Driver

<u>Interview with Lee with data
From Japanese friends</u>

The Careless Driver

The Careless Driver

It's Friday the 21st of April, and we have Lee (says his name to recorder). And he's native to Japan. Oh, I'm native to Nashville, but I read about stuff from all over the world. (Fact checked later his data as correct) Some of this stuff is from what my friends from Japan have told me. Okay, this is third-hand knowledge, but we'll take it anyway because it's better than any data I've read yet—I'll probably fact-check this. (According to Lee, Japan when certifying or registering drivers, each applicant is expected to spend 2-3000 dollars U.S. on education classes, drive school. Which I find absolutely astonishing, compared to the United States. In addition, new drivers are tagged with a symbol on their windshield[2]1 with a flower, and the flower is called? It's called a Wakaba* mark, a yellow and green sort of thing. It looks like a butterfly; one side or wing is green, and one is yellow. Very distinctive and old people/drivers get a marker and how old do they have to be? I'm going to look at that now...it says 75 and over. All right, that's good— seventy-five and over, O.K. But if they are 70 and they have a condition that could affect their driving, they have to display it too.

---

[2] This sticker or emblem must stay on the driver's windshield for a minimum of one year. More can be learned at https://99percentinvisible.org/article/wakaba-mark-japanese-car-stickers-signal-levels-driving-experience/

The Careless Driver

How did you come to know this knowledge—are you just interested in looking up things about Japan? That and just asking some Japanese friends. Oh, I see, just in conversation? Right. And I was just as shocked as you were when I heard when they told me it costs two thousand dollars, at least. Okay we'll look into that. (See fact-check, which I did, and it tallies exactly). Just the fact that you mentioned that this is a practice, this isn't just a one-shot deal, for one person who has had an accident. This is a *practice for all drivers in Japan.* That is astonishing. Yes.
**Wakaba translates to: "Green Leaf"

Yes, because we have (in the U.S.) our DUI syndrome where you wind up paying $5000.00 to $10,000 and you have to go, if not to prison, you have to go to some kind of community service, and you're probationary for the *rest of your life* (emphasized vocally but not true—only that the DUI never is erased from one's driving record, which was the intent of that remark. Right. So, we have our little scheme for *bad drivers.* (Note: Unfortunately, this is an after-the-act-scheme, which is a less than optimum method, since a number of DUI drivers are the cause of roadway fatalities. (Some 12,000 plus, in 2015[3], up

---

[3] Courtesy of our NHTSA at
https://crashstats.nhsta.dot.gov/Api/Public/ViewPublication/812317
Table 2

from 9, 943 in 2014--of which a percentage are repeat DUI / Alcohol Impaired drivers/offenders.)

We are at two and half minutes of this recording. I think we'll just cut it off. It's all we need...oh, no, I just spotted...what was the name of that flower again? W-a-k-a-b-a. (Lee iterates slowly and carefully.) Let's hear it for Wasabi! (Attempted humor) Lee and author both laughing. (Turned recorder back on) Lee just showed me the symbol for the elderly mark (for an elderly person, 75 years or above). Which is similarly colored but a four-leaf-clover. (Figure #2) Also, very distinctive. So, that wraps it up.

(Compare what your DMV or Public Safety Department requires to license fully a resident in your state compared with the requirements of Japan:)
(Excerpt from online blog regarding applying for Japanese driver license:) "After being issued my new paper license with a 6-month limit, a member of the staff at the center explained to me the next step. I needed to go out on the road at least 5 times with someone who had held a full driver's license for more than 3 years. Of course, the car needed to be manual too." – Road Training Section (Read full article at:)
(Gakuran, 2012) www.gakuran.com/driving-in-japan-passing-the-Japanese-drivers-test

The Careless Driver

(Figure 1) (A picture containing clip art showing a Wakaba: a Japanese emblem meaning "Green Leaf" assigned for one year to new drivers. Green on one half, Yellow on the opposite half. It looks similar to a butterfly and goes on back of car.)

(Figure 2) (A picture containing clip art showing a Koreisha: a Japanese emblem meaning "Elderly Person" assigned permanently to drivers who are 75 years old and above. In shape of a clover leaf, with four different colors, as a sticker on their automobile.)

(It is interesting and helpful to note that drivers from America and Brazil are required by law in Japan to take a test, to obtain a valid Japanese license, whereas

44

drivers from the United Kingdom and France are not required to be tested.) www.gakuran.com/driving-in-japan-passing-the-Japanese-drivers-test (Confidence in American drivers is not high in Japan, where their per capita death rate is less than half (5.2 per 100,000 persons) compared with America at 11.4 per 100,000.) https://www.who.int/health-topics/road-safety#tab=tab_1 Speaks of the heavy toll incurred in economic burden on the families of the deceased or injured party.

The Careless Driver

The Careless Driver

Interviews Texas & E. India

The Careless Driver

The Careless Driver

(Jim from Texas states that he drives an SUV. His training in TX did not include instruction on driving in rain or snow. Doesn't use gears in town to slow down vehicle. He mistakenly thought or was instructed that the time to shift to a lower gear is when his vehicle starts down a hill or slope. As for distance maintained behind vehicles on Interstates, he goes by experience, lengthens the usual distance when towing a trailer, and learned the 1 car length per 10 miles per hour rule from instructor.)

We're with Jim, heading toward Bridgestone Arena, downtown Nashville. It's 24th of May 2017, and he's about to answer the one question I ask all my individual riders, which is: Where did you first learn to drive? I think it was Indiana, high school drivers ed. course. Okay. How many practical hours in the seat, behind a moving vehicle did that education afford you? I have no idea. Take a rough guess, a wild guess. 40 hours. O.K. 40 hours, a lot more than usual. Now, do you recall what type of set-up you were in, in the car? Instructor in the passenger seat and three students in back seat. Really? Yeah, and then we rotated. You might find my story a little interesting: I lived in Indiana. Indiana did not have lottery tickets yet. So, every time I drove, I'm assuming since I was a decent driver, we drove to Illinois, so my Instructor could get lottery tickets. How interesting. (Jim is laughing.) And, when I drove, he always had a newspaper. One of our four guys drove *everybody*

The Careless Driver

paid attention. Yeah, let's just concentrate on your education...So, were there dual controls in the car? Did he (instructor) have control? He had a brake. Okay, all right. Do you recall any of the instructions he gave you at the beginning that stand out? I don't remember getting much. He just let you drive for practice? Yeah. And he was just monitoring that? Yup. Did you go on the Interstate? Yeah. Good—did you go on the Interstate during rush hour? Yep. How about during rain? Probably. Okay, probably. That's a 50/50. Yeah. All right, did he teach you how to back the car up correctly? We did, we did parallel parking. (not the same) Parallel parking, no back-up. Did he tell you how to handle a skid? Yeah! He did that. Okay, did he try to simulate that (maneuver) anywhere, even in a parking lot? No. No. O.K. I'm finding most of the instructors never do that. It was in the summer. If it had been in the winter.... Possibly, that would be more appropriate. How about yield and stop signs, did he give you explicit instructions on what they are and how to handle them. Yeah. He did? O.K.
What about following distance, on the Interstate—your car in back of another car? Most of the time he was reading the paper a lot. So, no real instruction on that. Interesting. O.K. Well, this will all go into the book. All right, how would you rate yourself (as a driver) right now on a scale from 1-10, here in Nashville? 9? Good, and why is that? I had a job where I was commuting 150 miles a day. In Chicago.

The Careless Driver

In Chicago. Miles of experience driving in Chicago traffic. Was this a normal car vehicle or was this a truck... No, was a car. Was this in the city proper-with traffic and lights and... Traffic, lights in suburbs...Great. In Indiana, even beyond driver's ed., even before you can get your license, they have to have a hundred hours on their own. They have a sheet. Every time they drive, we put our initials as a parent. They drove two hours here, three hours there. We must accumulate a hundred hours before they can get their license. Good, good. And have you done this with your children? And have you included rush-hour Interstate driving? I'd say some Interstate. Never have then drive in Chicago rush-hour. Okay. My wife would have a heart attack. Now, you are speaking about Chicago as if you—is that your home base? Southwest Indiana. And actually, that Interstate is one of the busiest Interstates in the country. I don't doubt it. So, living here is temporary? I'm on business. End of interview.

So, this is Varsha from India (with heavy accent): which section of India, province? M----------, (E. Indian pronunciation for Central India. Central, that's what I wanted. So, my first question to you is: What are the requirements for a citizen of Central India to get a driver's license? (Her answer begins with an unintelligible set of words-then:) passport, I remember only that. What about your driving skills?

The Careless Driver

Yeah, I have passed road test. <u>Are you required to take any formal training at a training...</u>Yeah, at a training center I have passed my training. <u>Can you briefly describe what training you received at this training school—what type</u>...did they take you out on fast roads like the super-highways. <u>Do they have super-highways in India, or are they just highways?</u> Highways. <u>And how often do they take you out and train you?</u> Daily, for one month. <u>Do they teach you how to handle a car if it is on a rainy day and it skids?</u> Ya. <u>They did!?</u> Ya. <u>Did they try to make you step on the brake and make the car skid or they told you how to handle it? (Doesn't quite get the question.) Did you skid the car *yourself*?</u> Ya. <u>What was the result?</u> I passed to my test. <u>Okay, let's go back before the skid. When I say skid, I'm talking about a plane, a car starts to move by itself in a certain direction without control. That's a skid.</u> Okay. <u>That's from because the water is on the asphalt. Water is on the road.</u> Okay. <u>And the car starts to go out of control. That's a skid. You didn't do that?</u> I didn't do that. <u>No. And, in training they didn't tell you what to do when the car begins to go out of control because it's on water?</u> No. <u>No, O.K. Did they tell you how to take a sharp turn?</u> Ya. <u>Okay, did you practice that?</u> Ya. <u>You did. How many times? One time, two times, three times (etc.)</u> I don't remember. <u>O.K., do you think it is less than five times?</u> Ya. Okay, thank you. (Language difference, and her accent

The Careless Driver

definitely a barrier.) (3 minutes 30 seconds into interview) (Pause recording)
What were some of the other skills the instructor taught you about driving? I would have (undecipherable word). (Note: Upon going over the audio of this short section about fifty times, it may be that she replied:) My other skills? (That seems to be her response.) Yeah, other abilities, other duties of a driver—what was the instructor telling you to do as a driver, during this 30-day period? So...(Varsha tries to recollect...) So, every day you went out, in a car, and an instructor, Ya. Teacher was here (Interviewer points to passenger seat.) Ya. Did they have dual controls? Ya. (She's certain.) Good, so he was taking you through certain neighborhoods and teaching you certain things—what did he teach you mainly? How to drive...Yes, but specifically? What things, how to come to a stop at a stop light, a stop sign? Yeah about a stop line. Okay, did he teach you about speed laws, or how to adjust your speed when it is raining or snowing? When I was taking the training, it was no rain. Okay, thirty days, no rain. All right, What about other traffic, cross-traffic. Did he teach you how to look for oncoming cross traffic at an intersection? Yeah...to see back and forth, right and left, and then I *list speed*. (Here she means I check speed.) Now, when it comes to turning the vehicle on a sharp turn, what did he tell you to do there? Less speed. At what point) did he tell you to do that? Starting of turn.

53

The Careless Driver

<u>Starting of turn?</u>! (Proper is before turn and speeding up gradually in the turn so that passengers and driver are not thrown by centrifugal force against doors or each other.) <u>He didn't say *before the turn?*...</u> Before the turn. <u>Oh, before the turn. O.K. good. What about yielding. Traffic coming in on the right or the left. Yielding to traffic?</u> In India, left side must, and right side must. Yield far left side, in India.
<u>They must yield for left.</u> (Note: Like the U.K. vehicles in India drive on *left* side of roadway. (For me, must stop. [40 second phone call delay.]) <u>Did the instructor have you back up the vehicle a distance?</u> Ya. <u>Good.</u> (Taking my passenger through her home gate.) End. (<u>Note:</u> The main point here is that East Indian citizens who want to drive legally must undergo a minimum of *thirty* days of instruction from a qualified driving instructor.)

The Careless Driver

Interviews with Amy (Alabama)
Tim (NC) and Levi (OH)

The Careless Driver

The Careless Driver

Okay, we're jawing here with Amy on the way to 410 Union Street, downtown Nashville, on the 25th of May 2017. Tells me her daddy taught her, (in Alabama) some things. Not a whole hell of a lot but, one main thing stuck in her mind: Keep it between the mustard and the mayonnaise. For those who are not familiar with Alabamaneese, we're talking about the double yellow and the broken or white line. MAYONNAISE AND MUSTARD. And, then she got some schooling in high school in a simulator car, not the real thing. She definitely didn't take the car out on the Interstate, and definitely not during rush-hour. Is that right? (Nods, yes.) You received no professional training or paid for training from a driving school? (No.) So, when you are driving how would you rate yourself on a scale of 1 to 10 as a driver? ("A six," was Amy's answer.) Have you skidded a car on purpose, just to see how to handle it? When did you do that? It was raining on a little back road one night, just wanted to know if I could, so I did.

How did it turn out...when you skidded the car? I'm still here. Yeah, but what happened to the car?! Nothin' Oh, nothing? Straightened right up. Did you go in a circle? Yes. And nobody else was around? Yep. (Proudly.) Excellent. Have you been told how to handle a skid in the future? I think you're supposed to—if you're going left you hit the wheel to the right. Something like that. Opposite...(Note: Amy thought

57

The Careless Driver

she should turn in the opposite direction of the skid.) (Corrected that notion.) And you take your foot off the gas at the same time. Gotcha. Okay, so that's something she didn't know—or she had skewered in her brain. I've had other drivers say the same thing by the way in similar interviews. Okay, now, when you go on the Interstate here in Nashville or in Tennessee, tell me how that goes—what do you do? I don't drive here at all. Very clever woman—I wouldn't either. Why would I when I can get dropped off at the front door (Laughs). Don't have to pay for parking. Yeah, parking (expense) can kill ya. Okay, so that's the extent of your education, simulator and Dad, on the back roads of Alabama. O.K. Cool, thank you.

We're here with Tim, at the International Airport, Nashville. And he's originally from North Carolina, or was in N.C. and moved to Tulsa, OK. And, was raised in Springfield, Texas, and that is where his dad. Well, first of all he was go-carting and riding motorcycles—what type of motorcycle did you ride? Suzuki 80. So, it was almost like a moped—kinda small, right? Yeah, small. Kinda easy? It was a pretty mean dirt bike for a small. Oh yeah, for a dirt bike. Oh yeah, they can be mean. So, it was a dirt bike, not a moped type thing. So, he learned how to control *a vehicle* at the age of 12 or 13. Which is great. Dad took Tim on a trip to...from Tulsa to...from Springfield Texas...to the Carlsbad Caverns, 200 miles approximately. Mexico?

The Careless Driver

Mexico. <u>After that, did you get in school, did you get driver education in high school?</u> I did, I did in Homestead, Florida. My driver's education was my wrestling coach. I was able to drive just fine on the road. We got our miles in, but it was pretty lay-back. <u>Did he take you on any of the major U.S. highways or Interstates?</u> He did, with little tips along the way. <u>Can you tell me about the little tips and pointers?</u> Uh...It is hard for me to remember specifics it's been so long ago. (<u>Note:</u> This is where I use a skill, developed as an interviewer to help persons recall better—it works and is a lot of fun.<u>)</u>

<u>First of all, do you have a picture of his face?</u> I don't, no. <u>Okay, so in your mind?</u> Oh, yeah, a picture in my mind. <u>O.K. great. Now, how many hours would you say he drove with you?</u> All total, about two or three hours. <u>Really? Was there any other education after that, either professional or paid for, or let's say a friend who was a really classy driver?</u> No. <u>So, its father at 12/13, and this three hours or so from this instructor in high school?</u> Yeah. <u>Interesting....End.</u>

<u>Levi:</u>
(Headed to The Turnip Truck (a whole foods type of grocery market), to have a holistic breakfast. He's from Ohio.) <u>My first question is: Where did you first learn how to drive a car or truck?</u> I first learned from mother in Ohio. <u>What age?</u> (Here the recording skips)

59

The Careless Driver

<u>On surface streets, in a parking lot, on an Interstate or rural road?</u> Yeah, I had to wait until I got my permit. <u>Mom was sitting next to you? How many hours would you say your mom put in?</u> Many. (There's a break in the recording at this point [unknown cause] continued with:) <u>If you had to put a number on the hours behind a wheel with an instructor, what would that number come out?</u> Gosh, my memory is a little foggy...I know it hit state guidelines. Off the top of my head I'd say 50.

<u>Let's talk state guidelines—when you were growing up and learning how to drive—what are we talking about there?</u> I don't know what they are either. <u>O.K, so you had fifty with a professional instructor, dual controls?</u> Ah, no. <u>Just sitting next to you, like mom?</u> Hmm, hm. <u>Did you go out on the Interstate—how many times?</u> Again, it's fifteen years, I don't remember off the top of my head, I remember being on the Interstate. <u>Ever in the rain or snow?</u> I don't remember if it rained, I don't remember either one, but I would say there's a better chance of rain than snow due to the time of season that I was in. <u>Can you give an idea of what the instructor stressed in the instruction period?</u> (Thinks.) We went over everything. So, went over...(not coming to him). <u>What salient points did he go over that you can remember?</u> (Slowly thinking...) Put your hands...<u>Like the old ten and two (positioning)?</u> Yeah—just what to do and the red light,

The Careless Driver

turn you know, and...I mean we just went through different, every scenario you'd want to teach. Again, I'm not giving you good data. Well I'll ask some questions to see if something pops up—what about following the car ahead—distance and speed? Yeah, we went over that. Do you recall anything about that, that you use today? No. How about handling merge signs and merging onto the Interstate or getting off the Interstate? I know we went over it. I don't remember anything that's valid. Okay. You drive now, right? Yes. And what type of vehicle? I drive a very old SUV. Okay, how old is *very old?* Mid-nineties. O.K and how often do you do that? I live about a tenth of a mile from where I work. So, I walk or bike to work most days. But, you know, if I ever—I might drive a car a couple times a week. Do you ever rent a car and take a long trip? (Boy is this showing interest or what?) No, not really. Okay, well great. Thank you for your comments. Absolutely. End.

The Careless Driver

The Careless Driver

Interview with Rajat (India) and
Ryan (Tennessee)

The Careless Driver

The Careless Driver

Rajat:
(From memory, not a recording) It's the morning of June 2nd, and I've just dropped off Rajat. He's from Nepal, and he's already given up driving here in Nashville, or at least in the United States for a while because he had an accident. He doesn't even know how it happened. Wasn't rain. Wasn't on the Interstate. Wasn't at nighttime. So, I quizzed him about, we only had a little bit of time. I quizzed him about what it takes to get a license legally in Nepal. He said you take a test of about 20 questions and you drive on a pre-determined route, doing left turns, right turns, using signals, backing up and so forth. That's about it. So, I asked him, who taught him. He says, well it was another newbie. Another beginner driver, which confirms my suspicions about the trouble here in Nashville (and other cities), is that they are under-trained. End.

Ryan: (Not recorded.) When and where did you learn to drive? I'll tell you something if it's not recorded. (Ryan wanted to go off record) Ryan's mother when he was age 14 took him out a few times in a parking lot and had him drive around. Then he got Driver's Ed. in high school. He thinks maybe 8 hours on the road...but this was with *Brentwood Training Program*. (See "Phil" an instructor's interview at beginning of book.) Schooled in Knoxville, TN. (He's an accounting major from UT.) The school (High school is

65

understood here.) did take him out on the Interstate. He didn't specify whether it was or not in rush hour. He did say, one of the last things they would have him do is take him out on the Interstate, otherwise they wouldn't pass, because they (Brentwood students need skills before they go out onto a major highway, like an Interstate which requires a little more confidence. His driver took him out on Interstate but not during rush hour. That's the *last* test, since students would fail without prior experience driving in general, Ryan disclosed.)

The Careless Driver

Interviews with John (KS) and
Thomas (TX), Plus Elaine, Chris, and Rajiv

The Careless Driver

The Careless Driver

John:
(Tells us how he got his start driving in Kansas—now residing in Nashville, in Dad's countryside pickup truck at age 14.) I grew up in the country in Kansas far away from pretty much everything. Driving my dad's pickup truck allowed me to go to school or work. <u>Okay, this was a standard shift, on the column?</u> It was "Three on the tree" (A saying I've never heard) <u>And did you teach yourself most of time, or did your father spend time with you?</u> My dad spent most of the time with me and even when I would sit on his lap, he would let me steer the car while he gave it the gas. I also worked a lot mowing lawns and pastures, driving tractors, and things like that. Internal combustion most of my life. <u>And, as you got into the later part of your school life, high school, was there an education program where you went out with an instructor?</u> I did like, I think it was a standard driving thing to get my license. <u>What did that consist of?</u> Driving with a person, like an instructor, kinda standard what a driving experience would be. How to parallel park, all your signs, braking, turn signals. Not performance driven though. <u>What type of hours do you think were involved with that instruction?</u>

Some while ago, if I can remember, something like they would pick me up at school. They would show up after my high school was done and I would go for maybe an hour or two, couple times a week, for about for about a month. <u>So, total hours about 10?</u> I say 10-20 hours.

<u>Any other instruction, either professional or non?</u> None. Felt pretty confident behind the wheel. <u>Okay, great. And you've driven outside of Tennessee, right?</u> I have, yes. <u>Have you gone on any trip longer than 100 miles?</u> Yes, many times. <u>And in your vehicle?</u> Huh, huh. <u>How would you rate yourself on a 1-10 scale as a driver?</u> Like as far as safety...<u>Confidence as a driver.</u> I would say an "8-10". <u>When getting on the Interstate during rush hour,</u> which you have done, right? Yes. <u>Describe to me how you do it.</u>

Depending on how much traffic there is, if there's a lot of traffic, try not to be close to anybody (John said "everybody"), because it will bottleneck... (garbled words) a lot of times. Make sure you have space between you and other drivers. You kinda have to just eyeball and watch the traffic that is already on the highway. Who else is in front of me, and wait for a gap to come in. If you see an opening, have to adjust your speed, try to match theirs, signal them and merge.

O.K. John, so you look for an opening and you try and match the speed and you merge? Correct. <u>Good. How would you define the word merge?</u>

The Careless Driver

How would I define it? Well, in a car we don't have verbal communication with other drivers, so we use things like turn signals. We can use our hands to wave, make eye contact with somebody, it's kinda different in every situation...but it's just one of those things that just kinda happens. Both drivers that are involved in the merge are paying attention. Sometimes they're not. It's also judging to if you are merging in, you have to think about how fast the other person (driver) is going, and what the performance limitations are of your car. Should I speed up to get in front of him/her or are they going too fast. Should I wait and fall in behind, that kinda thing. <u>Notice:</u> <u>Up until now the definition of *merge* he has not simply stated.</u> (This *lag in answering* is a sign that the word and its meaning are not well understood, and so poses a hazard to and by drivers who have never defined the word yet encounter it almost daily. In high speed travel, any traffic flow, this is unacceptable.) <u>How would you define the word *merge*?</u> The coming together of two things. In the sense of driving it's two cars coming together in the same lane. (Unfortunately, that definition would also apply to two vehicles colliding with each other—you see my meaning?) <u>And **then**, John qualifies his definition thus:</u> But they can't occupy the same space. <u>How do you take turns at high speed—let's say you are going south on I-65 (a North / South highway) and you see, ah 440 (East/West). I want to go over to</u>

The Careless Driver

<u>Green Hills. It says (speed limit) 45 mph. Or 21st (Ave.) Yeah.</u> It's also depended on traffic, that turn. I know is a very kinda wide gradual turn. My particular car is very low to the ground, so it has a very good center of weight (the term is *center of gravity*). The suspension is also rather tight. So, I know on those kind of turns, because I know the feeling of my car, I don't have to slow down a ton. Now, if I were driving an SUV that has a higher center of weight, something like that, kinda feel it roll a little bit.

<u>At what point to you begin to slow down? (This question asked of another driver I interviewed earlier.)</u> I'm usually coming into a corner like that will let off the gas just before I even start to take the turn. Start to coast. And then maybe tap on [my] brakes just to let the person behind you know that you are slowing down. And, if you just let off the gas, they might not recognize you are slowing down? So, you can signal them with your brakes and your turn signal. Once I'm into the turn kinda judgmentally judge what it is going to look like, I will slowly start putting on the accelerator again and push through the turn if I'm going a little too fast. End.
*(Not necessary at all. It gives a false signal to drivers behind who should also be trained and aware that the slowdown occurs well before the turn.)

The Careless Driver

<u>Thomas</u>: (For brevity, several of Thomas's answers are given in short. He's from Texas. Parents funded driver training.) <u>How many hours on the road with instructor?</u> I'd say in Texas. <u>High school?</u> No, just part of getting license go to driving school. <u>How many hours?</u> 12 to 20 hours. <u>Drove Interstate?</u> Yeah, I did. <u>Did you get a chance to drive in the rain or rush hour?</u> We drove in heavy traffic. (Rates himself on scale 1 to 10 a "7" as a driver. Drives a small SUV.) <u>Do you ever go through the gears to slow the vehicle down?</u> Not in town. <u>Did you understand the fact that the gears speed up and slow down the car—you observed that yourself or did your teacher teach you that?</u> My instructor taught me that.

<u>What is the best time to shift to the lower gear?</u>[4] Before you go down a hill. (True. Also, upon slopes upward and inclines, carrying a heavier load/weight than usual it is safe to manually using sequential gears go to higher gears since the slope automatically slows the vehicle so that a smooth transition and more slowing is obtained. Same for flat roads and highways, when in heavy traffic and your car is an SUV.)

---

[4] Lower gear here means turning *slower* because it is a larger (diameter) gear, usually lower in number also.

The Careless Driver

Have you seen when you are driving, have you seen drivers who stop at yield signs unnecessarily. Not sure, maybe.
When you are on any Interstate how do you maintain distance from your vehicle to the vehicle in front—what do you use as a guide? I probably just use experience now, but, when towing a trailer, I use more, if not I use less, as I was taught to do. One car length per second (Use what? On this specified question responding with vague answer is not a good sign that he has been trained properly—then he corrects himself): Sorry, one car length per 10 miles per hour. That was the standard. Then it became two seconds. Like if you [vehicle in front] passes a pole, or some kind of marker—you pass it two seconds or later that was good. Now they have upped it to three. Which shows the deterioration in perception of our driving community. If that is not an indictment, I don't what is. What's your opinion of these signs, these neon or traffic notification signs that keep saying how many people are dying on our Interstates or highways? I think some of that is good. I don't love the *cheeky* ones...they make driving seem trivial. There's a couple of good ones, but most are flat, don't have much meaning or punch. I wish there were more positive—like the "Please keep Nashville litter free, instead of "Don't Litter/$100 Fine. The former is an appeal to the positive side of life. Instead of always telling people "Don't do this. Don't do that." People get so,

74

The Careless Driver

<u>it's a hard response to the word "Don't" that after a while it becomes ineffective altogether. End.</u>

(Driving to taco restaurant with Elaine on Thursday: she tells me that there is 200 hours of driver training, behind the wheel in the state of New Hampshire plus theory.) (Note: New Hampshire has the lowest traffic fatality rate per capita of any of the 50 states.) <u>Continue.</u> Then actual course work, you had three or four months. You had classroom hours then additionally to classroom hours you had more behind the wheel driving time with the instructor. <u>In your 200 hours, were you taught how to yield properly?</u> Yes. <u>Taught not to follow too closely?</u> Yes. <u>Were you given a chance to skid the car, let's say in a parking lot, where it wouldn't hurt other people just to handle a skid?</u> They had us drive through a parking lot of snow to get what it felt like (garbled). <u>Fantastic. None of what you told me is done here in Nashville.</u> <u>If it snows, they don't take the students out, if it's raining they don't take the students out on the Interstate or even out on the highways.</u> How are they going to learn? <u>That's why the book is being written.</u> <u>So, how many hours of classroom?</u> Three months, and one class two or three times a week. Then separate from those classroom days, that's when you would set up schedule days to go out and drive thirty to forty-five-minute period. You had to have a certain number of those scheduled with an instructor.

The Careless Driver

Chris:
(It's Sunday, 28 May 2017)
(He just told me he had a fender bender on Granny White at the corner of Tyne Blvd, which is a four-way stop, and it was raining yesterday. The car hydroplaned down from 35/40 mph and hit another car in the intersection.) Where did you first learn to drive? Knoxville, TN, rural roads at age 15. First license? 16. Did you have any formal training in high school or otherwise? Yeah, I took a driving class. And how long were you behind the wheel in that driving class? (At first not sure, said 4 hours) Less than twenty hours. Did you have an instructor on the passenger side with dual controls? Yes. What were some of the main things he tried to instill in you as a driver, newly? The usual things, proper speed, that kind of stuff. Did you go out on the Interstate several times? I think so. Interstate 40? Yes. Did he have you back the car up any great distance? We did parallel parking. (No backing up.) How about going out in the rain or rush hour—not that Knoxville has much of a rush hour compared to us/Nashville? We were in traffic; I don't think rush hour. Moderate traffic. How do you handle yield signs, going on the Interstate—tell me about the speed of your car? Actually, merging onto the Interstate, I would be aiming to be up to Interstate speed. Do you ever slow down or stop for the left-hand lane? No. (That was all the time we had for the interview in the car.)

The Careless Driver

Rajiv:
(Started with dad, 1998. No formal instruction after that.) Start with a standard shift or automatic? (Says it wasn't a new car so standard. Standard but now drives an automatic. Not a sport automatic.) (There's a lot of road noise on this recording making it difficult to transcribe exactly his words.)

How about in high school, were you given any training or classes? Yeah, I did take driver's ed. What did that consist of? We had a driver's ed. car, dual controls. Where and when would they take you? We'd drive around the city. No interstate practice, or in the rain/snow? Teach you how to skid a car? No. Did they teach you merging and getting off properly from a highway? No...
I'm discovering that there are a lot of under-educated drivers in this country, with hand-me-downs from dad and Uncle Joe. (Rajiv agrees.)

The Careless Driver

The Careless Driver

<u>Interview with
Trevor (Buffalo, NY)</u>

The Careless Driver

The Careless Driver

Trevor:
(Driving with Trevor from Buffalo, New York. Recently moved down to Vanderbilt area - Nashville.) <u>Where and when, and who taught you how to drive?</u> "The first time I drove a car was on a Saturday morning right after I had gotten my permit at the DMV in Buffalo. My dad gave me the keys...baptism by fire, I was 16 years old. He handed me the keys...sure enough I didn't know that as soon as you take the car out of park, put it in drive, if you don't have your foot on the gas it starts moving a little bit. That kind of sent me through a loop. On the 15-minute drive home I was heavy on the brake. First time I drove a car and learned from experience. <u>When did you first attempt to get on an Interstate?</u> "Probably two or three months after that. <u>Was that I-95 or 90? What difficulties do you sometimes encounter during Interstate rush hour traffic?</u> Coming from a smaller city, just volume, especially the Interstate I'm accustomed to, the stretch on 90, in Western New York is only two lanes, east and west bound. If a truck ever needs to pass, that can get a little dicey because there are only two lanes. <u>What is your reaction—what do you do, your mental process?</u> Generally, I'll try and pass trucks before they pass me. <u>When there are no trucks, how do you judge the distance between you and the car ahead?</u> In New York we have a set of mile markers in the middle of the Interstate. (Garbled words.) They have 3 posts

between every tenth mile. So generally, the rule of thumb, you want to say...one car length per second. (He meant per 10 mph.) (Also note his answer came *hesitantly* – and that as stated earlier is not a good indicator of skill or adequate for reaction time on highways.) That's the original one. The new one they came out with several years ago: you pick out a post or a sign and you count like that red truck, (author indicating) one thousand one, one thousand two, one thousand three. And expect to be three of those (3 seconds) between you and the car ahead. But that's good, one car length per 10 mph is good. (Certainly, much more than is allowed on Interstates that I have traveled.) (Learned on an automatic with Dad—same type transmission now. Drives a Honda CRV.)

Do you use gears to slow the down vehicle? If it's heavy rain, I'll put it in low gear. How about city traffic? We don't have much city traffic up there, so generally don't have to. When it comes to merging onto the Interstate 90? New York has toll booths on every entrance and exit. Obviously, there's the branches like 190, 290, 390...There's no just clear getting on ramp? There is generally, it's just a longer third lane comes off the toll plaza. For getting off the highway? You try to get up to speed, with everybody else and then shift over. The general rule of thumb is if you see someone trying to merge on, obviously if it

The Careless Driver

is safe for you to move into the left and you're in the right lane. Just move over for him.
<u>What about emergency vehicles, do you have a law like we have here?</u> Yeah, State troopers and emergency vehicles: the law states you have to move over if safe. <u>Now, if there are no flashing lights on an emergency vehicle, what do you do?</u> If I see it parked on the shoulder and it's safe to move over, I'll generally always move over, regardless if I can see the maintenance worker, or whoever it might be. <u>Speaking of moving over, describe to me how you move from one lane to the left, the faster lane?</u> Generally, I check the review mirror, check the side mirror, over the shoulder, if that looks good, I move over. <u>What about signaling?</u> Oh yeah, of course signal before you check the mirror. <u>How long do you do that before you move over?</u> Generally, try to give it two clicks.

<u>What happens when you see an accident, emergency vehicles, a collision?</u> Tough to say, I haven't stumbled onto one. On a two lane, generally there's a lineup, I'm stopped before I see one. <u>Stopped?</u> I'll be in a line of cars. There will a be a line-up or a slowdown before I reach that point. <u>Always, always.</u>
<u>You're not a doctor or a medic-so there's nothing you can do about the injuries or collision, right?</u> If I were a witness to the accident, it happened immediately, I'd try to pass the scene of it, pull over where it is safe and try to help somebody out, and if it seemed I was

The Careless Driver

the first one to stumble upon the scene. I don't have medical training. <u>So, you would actually pull over?</u> Yeah, if I felt like I'd want to make sure that people were all right. <u>What if you were the tenth car?</u> And no one had pulled over? Probably pull over. (Note: Trevor qualified my question to him. At this point I had no more questions that were <u>not</u> oriented to Nashville driving conditions.) <u>I'll pause this now.</u> Sure, you will. You definitely care about this stuff. End.

The Careless Driver

Interview with Geeta and Glen

The Careless Driver

The Careless Driver

Geeta born in America, (Father born in India) <u>From whom did you learn to drive?</u> My brother in Texas at age 15. <u>Was this on a rural road, an Interstate, or a parking lot?</u> In an urban city on the side streets of our neighborhood. <u>With a permit?</u> Yes. <u>And what do you recall he mainly tried to stress in his instruction?</u> Safety #1, following the rules, and generally getting comfortable. Being a proactive driver. <u>What about speed?</u> Yeah, we talked about speed. <u>Well, what did he tell you to do about speed?</u> You know I don't recall anything specific about speed. <u>Would you say that you were always within the speed limit of the street that you were on?</u> Probably not. <u>You'd go with whatever the flow was, that pretty much is the covenant.</u>

<u>After that did you have any formal training after that?</u> I did. You have to go...<u>How many hours behind the wheel with an instructor?</u> I would say I did the course over a week. So, maybe three hours behind the wheel. <u>In that three hours did you go out on an Interstate highway?</u> No. <u>Did you drive in the rain?</u> Probably not. <u>Did you back the car up under supervision?</u> I did, yes. I definitely had to park and reverse back up, yeah<u>.</u> <u>So, what happens when you get on an Interstate now?</u> I only drive on the weekend. It was in Wash. D.C. <u>I-95 runs through there, did you get on the 95?</u> No. I go on 395 or Route 66 which are the two bigger highways a lot. <u>How do you handle the</u>

87

fast-moving traffic in the left lane as you come up on the merging lane? I only view to try to make sure I merge in appropriate spaces in the flow of traffic." What if there is a tractor-trailer on your left, doing about 65/70 (mph)? I sort of try to avoid large vehicles like that. Tell me about that, how do you avoid them? "I'll either try to go in front of them or the next lane over but directly not behind them. Have you ever stopped and waited on the shoulder 'til the truck passed? No, I think that would be very dangerous. End.

(Driving with Glen.) Where and when did you first learn how to drive? In Dallas, TX. I got my first permit when I was 15 and received my full license when I was 16. Do you drive daily? Yes. What difficulties do you sometimes encounter during Interstate rush hour traffic? People here, especially on this stretch we're about to get on, from Almaville Road to Hayward Lane, don't recognize the geographic anomalies in that stretch of road. Just the hills and the twists and turns, when people don't realize what lane they need to be in. Let's call them drivers. So, drivers aren't aware of terrain and rain, even though they've done this drive for the past five to ten years. They tend to put it on autopilot and react instead of plan. I've observed that. Give me an example of, recently when you've seen something like that, so we have something concrete for the book. So, the driver

The Careless Driver

yesterday-I drive pretty defensively, I watch out to see what another driver is going to do, and in really thick traffic I saw this guy in a red pickup cut across three lanes to get his exit. Really wasn't considering the whole picture? Yeah. Good, that's what I wanted, an example. I've seen this happen many times. In fact, two days ago I decided to put that into the book as well. You know, the changing of lanes after one click of the signal, or ½ click in heavy traffic of the turn (lane changing) signal and move over to another lane. Especially, a faster lane. Yeah! OK, let's go back to your beginnings, in Dallas. You got your permit what training did you get and from who? The school district put up portable trailers and we did driving simulations through the summer—two or three hours a day. Like in a parking lot? Yeah, in the parking lot in front of the high school. Me and nine other kids with this driving simulator that was really outdated from the '70's. But it put you in situations, grade you on your reactions. Almost, like a video game. Yeah, Yeah. How many hours do you think total? If it were a three-hour course Monday through Friday, probably did thirty hours of classroom in two weeks. Okay, what about in the simulator? That was the simulator. The rest was theory about traffic signs and lights and lanes and all that? And drunk driving and things like that. Now since that time, and before you got your full license, did you have any professional or other training from your parents or siblings? So, my dad and my brother-in-law: both took me out in their cars and let me practice driving on city streets. What type of traffic? Usually, after dinner so it would be a little lighter than day. Was the sun still out or was it night? With the sun starting to set. And then, practiced parallel parking, an element of the test. After the two weeks of classroom—you know I want to say it was one week in the classroom and one in the car. That's what it was. We're going back to the driver's ed. in high school? Yeah. I'll correct that, that's fine. We would get in the car where the instructor would sit where the passenger would sit. He would have his own brake pedal. Oh, so it went from simulator to real car? Yeah Oh, that's important. Yeah. Classroom slash simulator then car. But still under the control of the same environment, this tarmac--is flat area? We actually drove on highways. No Interstates, no I-90's, I-95's? I-65 in Dallas. But, not in rush hour? Not in rush hour. And not in the rain? And not in the rain. So, we practiced with the instructor behind the wheel. So, then brother-in-law, father, learning how to shift the manual transmission, parallel parking, is part of the exam with the state trooper.

How about backing up the vehicle a distance? Don't think I practiced that very much. All right. So, let's ask some poignant penetrating questions about you and the road when you're driving your Jeep Wrangler. What do you observe, and what do you use to guide

The Careless Driver

your vehicle as far as the vehicle in front of you on the Interstate? I do it by feel. I've been driving since, for 32 years. I like to be a safe distance behind the car in front of me. Tell me exactly about that, how you judge that: like an instance like this...I point to car ahead. This is a pretty good distance for me. Probably this is four car lengths? Do you know why I'm doing this? Because there is going to be slow-ups all along in this section here until after Thompson Lane. (Traveling on surface streets.) A part of the reason I do it in this lane is because drivers are going to want to merge over. Yeah, I also want to let drivers merge over and not have crunch time. So good, what rule of thumb that you've been taught do you use? There's a thing about every ten miles an hour you count a second. Right, do you still use that? I do it when I'm driving long distances, when I'm on cruise-control on the highway. Yeah, what about in this situation? This situation I just do it by feel. OK, give me an example the last time, yesterday or the day before—obviously, the traffic was no different. What would you say, let's say you are driving this car now, how close would you get to that car in front of the truck? I would get no closer than where that blue van is.

Blue van, blue van-oh, I see, blue van, if we moved it over. At this speed you would allow at least one car length? Definitely. OK, good. All right. What, and this is good, this is a good question because you are old enough to learn on a standard shift, the standard-shift your father was driving was a three-gear-Low, Medium, High, no six forward gears or five forward gears? Yeah. This may not apply, how about braking instead of gearing down to slow the vehicle? I learned how to gear down because my Dad says, He didn't want to pay to replace the brakes, although I guess replacing a transmission would be more expensive. (At this point the author did not interrupt Glen to note that using the vehicles transmission to gear down, if done properly, *does not wear out* the transmission.) What did father teach you about how to do that correctly? You know, man, it's been a long, long time...Because you don't drive a standard, do you? No, it's been a long time. OK, just take a moment, because there is a way with a 3-speed, low-medium-high, there is a way to do it properly. Probably, if you're just, like coming to a stop sign I would let the speed taper off, of its own volition, and then shift accordingly. Right, you would not do it on a downhill? You do not shift down to a lower[5] gear on a downhill. It's only done on an uphill. Yeah. That's empirical evidence I have already observed and put

---

[5]-Again, "lower" translates to larger slower turning gear. (Usually gears number 1 and 2 or (S") Note: Large/Heavy trucks do shift down to lower larger gears because of their weight and added momentum of that weight as they go downhill.

The Careless Driver

into the old vault of information on driving. Good! So, you came up with the right answer. Now, on a downhill you would go from Medium to High, or Low to Medium. There would be no real liability doing that. Right. You want to increase the speed or momentum of the car when you throw it into a higher *numbered* gear, you need more forward motion because the gears (that are working) are now smaller and they need more force to drive them. Like when you ride a multi-speed bicycle, you know how when you go to a lower gear your feet start doing this. (Demonstrating more push.) Right. Yeah. Good. All right, what have you observed about cars on the Interstate merging that stop on the merging lane for traffic to the left? Oh yeah, that's one of my-I've got many driving pet-peeves, but that is one of them. You don't stop on a lane, especially if...Cars behind...Yeah, if you have cars behind you, or you just take a risk and merge. Yeah, there's a little bit of a risk and the worst that can happen is you pull over into this lane here-the margin. (Author indicates the shoulder) It's really crucial. People just get terrified and kind of camp out at the end of the merge lane. OK, so fourth question: Also merging onto the Interstate more slowly than the traffic traveling in the immediate left lane—have you seen that? You see they come, kinda of drift over into the left lane, here in Nashville—if I were doing 60, 65 mph and they kind of drift over at 45 and 50 mph? Yeah, and they're not paying attention to the speed of

The Careless Driver

the traffic that they are flowing into. Yeah, good, OK. Now, what about changing lanes, well we just talked about this, changing lanes abruptly in heavy traffic, that's done. What do you do when you see flashing lights in an emergency vehicle on the right shoulder? You get at least one lane over. All right, that's the law... The other part is slow down to under 45 mph. But if it's *safe*, you are not forced to move over into this lane if they're on the shoulder, if it is safe, you don't do the thing we just talked about. You don't just pull over in front of another driver. I've seen that happen. What if there is an emergency vehicle stopped on the shoulder, the lights of the emergency vehicle aren't flashing? Any time there is a car in the right shoulder, I either change lanes or slow down to 45. If there is no flashing, you will attempt to get into the other lane? Yeah, because there is going to be a person present. OK, good enough. (The law in June of 2017 in Tennessee states exactly that, any type of vehicle that is in the margin.) Guess, we call that prudent driving. All right. When you see an accident coming up, there's been a collision, there's merging vehicles, there's police cars, what do you do—regardless of the amount of traffic—whether there's no traffic or whether there is very little traffic, what do you do? There's an accident, there is obviously some kind of kerfuffle...Yeah. on this side. I'm usually trying to get into the farthest lane away. In case there is an explosion or something. (Chuckles) Right, oh really?

The Careless Driver

Yeah. <u>All right. What if there is a slow-down, drivers are creeping by it, because they have some lurid interest in what's going on?</u> I hate that. <u>You have observed that many times, right?</u> Of course, yeah. <u>There's a weakness there. All right, left hand turners that turn too early into the oncoming traffic, not allowing for cars ahead (in opposite direction) to clear the intersection, have you seen that on surface streets? In other words, turning too soon[6].</u> Yeah, people not cognizant of the fact that there are oncoming cars. Drivers in Nashville generally are not cognizant, whether it is the landscape or other drivers. It is pretty frustrating. <u>Now, where do you look, where is your attention focused on the Interstate when you are driving—I know they say all around, on both sides and behind Keep the attention spanning. Where do you look 75% of the time?</u> I focus several car lengths. <u>As a rule?</u> Yeah. <u>As a rule—that's a good thing (practice). On a scale from 1 – 10, how would you rate your driving ability?</u> A nine. <u>Good.</u>

---

[6] Happened to author in 2017 in Nashville city proper at the corner of 4th Ave and Koreans Vets Blvd, forcing him to jam on his brakes with a car full of chauffeured passengers, ruining (warping) the front rotors—but no one was even discomforted.

The Careless Driver

The Careless Driver

Interview with Carlos (Philippines)

The Careless Driver

The Careless Driver

(Driving Carlos to BNA (International airport) from Franklin, TN. Carlos is from the Philippines, his dad taught him at age 12!) <u>What were the requirements when you were growing up to get a license?</u> Requirements where you could drive at age 15, with school four to five hours a day. <u>How many days?</u> Five hours a day back in the day, my youth. <u>I'll fact check that on the Internet.</u> (For the present requirements.) Five days a week. (Inaudible but recalled by interviewer.) You have to complete the course and then do like a test for learner's permit. <u>What did the test consist of?</u> Road signs, rules and all that. About 50 items. <u>What about driving?</u> You have to pass first, complete the test and then all the passes including the driving. <u>How many of the hours, five hours a day, 20 days are devoted to *behind the wheel?*</u> 10 sessions of driving takes one half hour each time. <u>In a simulator or actual car on street?</u> Actual car. <u>Do you ever go onto the major highways?</u> Yeah, you have to go first on the streets. Back then we don't honor the Stop. We don't have any Stop signs. The red stop-sign you have we don't have. (Really?!! I interject); Yeah! <u>Yeah! Is that still the case?</u> Not anymore. We have to really watch where we're going, a lot of people walking. I guess it's more a discipline...we're honoring now. You really need to be disciplined. Imagine four streets, four stops but there are no stop signs. <u>So now, you are on the streets in a car with the instructor here...do you have dual controls?</u> No. <u>Can</u>

The Careless Driver

the instructor stop the car? No. Can he steer the car? No, just me, just you alone. And it is a manual (transmission car). So, you're out for about a half an hour to an hour with this instructor who doesn't have control of car if you lose control? " Carlos responds with a Hmm Hmm (Yes).

Then you are on city streets without stop signs. Do you have traffic lights? Yes. And it's not in the rain, he doesn't take you out in the rain, does he? No. Does he (did he) take you out in rush hour? Yes, twice. Only twice, so, maybe it was only for about an hour? Yeah. It's hard. But you are still learning. And, if you stop sudden, they give you the horn. Right, so you're nervous, you don't want to mess it up? It's a manual transmission so sometimes you hit the wrong gear and you stop. You are panicking. How many hours did you dad work with you in the car? Every day. Every single day. What did your dad teach you? Mostly be patient and don't get hot-tempered. If you have some problems in the street and some person at your back blows his horn don't get rattled and mind your own business. What about taking turns at speed? Yeah, always observe your speed limit, always signal, left right. The textbook. In our DMV version you really have to follow the rules, or they will not pass you. Do you have 3 and 4 lane highways? Yes, similar to this I 65. Did father train you over and over again how to merge correctly onto the fast-moving-

The Careless Driver

<u>highway?</u> After I got my student permit. Yeah, 'because you can go there at 12 years old drive on the freeway if you have a professional licensed driver. Some do that, but my dad is from the military. <u>So, he would take you on the heavily trafficked highways and have you get on and get off?</u> Yes, when I got my learner's permit. <u>What did he teach you about following the car ahead of you?</u> Just mind your distance, I think 3 car lengths, you know, apart. Mind your distance apart, your speed, obviously all the time. <u>What kind of speed limits do you remember you had in those days?</u> Then? To tell you honest there also were no speed limits. <u>Really?</u> We're not following the limits...but there's one hundred percent, kilometers per hour so, like 60 on the streets...freeway, we call it highway, <u>100 kilometers?</u> Maximum, yeah, I think a hundred. <u>What difficulties did you encounter in your first year in rush hour traffic or heavy traffic, did you have any difficulties?</u> Yeah, the most trouble is the traffic and congestion, but there's a lot of cars on the road, and most of them are undisciplined, unskilled they just swerve wherever they want. We don't have we call it...officer? Back then that much. Late 80's. <u>Did you ever have a collision?</u> Never. I'm always getting accidents here...getting my rear ended. <u>Oh yeah?</u> Yeah, mostly stopping, like you know, freeway? Fortunately, not so hard so, but too close to you. <u>Yeah, following too close-I find that's one of the major weaknesses.</u> That's why I keep my distances.

The Careless Driver

<u>Yeah, look what I'm doing-ten car lengths behind vehicle in front.</u> And my son, who is 14 now always tailgates. I tell him: When it's time to do your driving keep the distance that I have. Don't follow too close. You never know when the guy in front of you stops. <u>Yeah, either you'll hit him, or someone will hit you.</u> End.

The Careless Driver

<u>Interview with Allison (North New Jersey)
Marissa (Chicago)</u>

The Careless Driver

The Careless Driver

Allison:
(We're traveling to the Johnny Cash Museum on the tenth of June '17 with Allison from North New Jersey)
<u>Who was the first person who helped you to learn how to drive?</u> My cousin's girlfriend. (Erin) <u>Your age at the time?</u> Sixteen, in my town and she brought me to my middle school. And, we learned how to drive, and how a car behaves in a parking lot. <u>This is before you had a permit, right?</u> Yes. <u>Now, after that did you get any formal training in high school or from a professional driver?</u> I had to do three or two classes for six hours with a training driver. <u>Was it a driver training school?</u> _Yeah. A driver training service. <u>What did that person help you to learn?</u> (Smiling / cheerfully spoken) Well, the first thing they did is take me out to the highway in Hoboken (N.J.) So that was gotten right in. <u>Good old Hoboken, what highway is that?</u> 80...<u>During rush hour?</u> No. <u>And, not during the rain, right?</u> No.
<u>What are some of the [points] that you can recall?</u> Blinkers (signals), braking...<u>What about the flow of traffic merging?</u> Yeah, merging (she's recalling) <u>How often did he teach you to go on and off?</u> Don't remember (still cheerful) <u>You say six hours behind the wheel?</u> Yeah, we did two, two and two (hours) <u>Excellent, what about the car you are following ahead of you – give you a rule to work with?</u> A car or two behind. (Note: this is insufficient gap for any normal

105

The Careless Driver

highway scenario.) Did he attach any significance to your speed? (Lag here in replying) (So, I coached a bit.) Because the old rule is one car length for every 10 mph. Yeah, I'm sure that was it. (Laughs) That was it—I'm helping your recall. That's fine. (Allison is laughing.) And, what about taking turns at speeds—like we're coming up to a fairly sharp turn? To slow down...When did he tell you to do that? When I was turning because I didn't listen. I drove with my mom after that I sped up around a turn (a few garbled words here.) You know, it's O.K. to speed up once you are in the turn? (She acknowledges knowing that.) Okay, tell me about these questions—I've got a couple of canned questions for Tennessee drivers. What difficulties do you sometimes encounter during Interstate rush-hour traffic? More traffic--not happy, especially New Jersey. You've got the hands and the swearing (undecipherable). Well, that's the influence of New Yorkers, probably.[7] Going on the shoulder...Really, to get around? Yeah. Tell me about [drivers] changing from the right lane to the faster left lanes—an incident if you recall it. (She mentions the habit of putting on directional signals but not waiting before changing but just changing lanes.) During rush hour? I have found that here a bit in Nashville. They put on their blinker *as they are changing lanes.* Or they don't do that at all. What about following the

---

[7] Author was raised in New York City and suburb.

The Careless Driver

vehicle too closely in front, do you see that in New Jersey? Yeah. (Author acknowledges and that it happens a lot here in Nashville.) What about SUVs, following behind these [wide] SUVs in your Jetta? Yeah... Kind a hard to see (much ahead), Yeah, you don't know how the traffic is going. Now, how have you normally kept your attention on the road ahead—where do you keep it mainly? I like looking in the rearview mirror a lot. And a lot!? Why is that—you are heading forward—you think you might get rear-ended? YES.

Did that happen? Yeah once, which is probably why. All right let's go back *before* the rear-end. Where did you put your attention in terms of distance on the Interstate? (Allison indicates just the car ahead.) Now, you know the way to do it is to look five to ten cars ahead, so you can tell the flow of the traffic, right—you've been taught that haven't you? (Laughs. Apparently not.) Of course, that's when the big SUVs get in the way and make it impossible to see. All right, number two: did you learn from your cousin's friend on an automatic transmission or a manual one? (Automatic-never has driven a manual transmission.) Even in your automatic (Jetta made by Volkswagen) you have, I'm pretty sure, sequential gears, tell me about that. It didn't really go well—it would just do it if I didn't do the right thing. Well, do you have any knowledge or instruction on how to slow a car down

The Careless Driver

<u>using the gears?</u> (she answers no.) <u>Therefore, you don't do that?</u> No. <u>Yeah, most drivers don't know or don't do that.</u>

<u>How about have you ever seen a driver stop on a merging lane onto an Interstate?</u> (She indicates that she has.) <u>How often would you say you've seen that the number of times you've been on the Interstate.</u> (She indicates several.)

<u>How about too slowly onto the Interstate or slower than the traffic?</u> (Again, she indicates yes.)
<u>What do you do as a driver when you see an emergency vehicle?</u> Pull over. (I had to further find out what she meant here.) Get over to the next lane.
<u>When there is an accident on the *other side* of the Interstate, do you slow down for that?</u> (Note her answer here.) Everybody does. They're so curious. <u>Yeah, not a good thing.</u> (Unless one enjoys more rear-ends, traffic tie ups and slows than usual.) <u>What would you really want to do in that situation?</u> Get going. <u>That's right move over and get out of that area.</u>
(Note: When we *really think about it,* Interstates have no stop signs and no traffic lights. There should never be a slow-down to a point where the cars come to a stop. Completely unnecessary.)

The Careless Driver

<u>Have you seen left hand turners turn too soon into the oncoming lane?</u> (Again, she indicates this is something that she has observed.) (At this point Allison's destination is coming up so I end the recording and thank her for her candid replies and data.)

(Using sequential gears in any car or SUV going up a slope or hill is advisable. For one, downshifting increases control that is lost when simply braking, and in wet conditions this could prove pivotal to the stability of the vehicle and thus the safe transport of its occupants. Two, in conjunction with the slowing effect of the incline, gravity, and braking simultaneously can avoid collision with a large vehicle in front that has come to nearly a stop, such as a fully loaded tractor-trailer or fully loaded bus. Conclusion: the use of gears, sequential in an automatic or standard transmission also to slow a vehicle is not only for navigating down slopes.)

(Marisa from Chicago, visiting Nashville, born in upstate New York. She like a lot of drivers I've interviewed got started driving with her dad.) <u>Was it in a parking lot or on a street?</u> In a parking lot. <u>Did you start with a manual shift or an automatic?</u> Started with a manual. <u>You'd be surprised how many women have been taught by their fathers to start with a manual. Back in Chicago, what do you notice about drivers following too closely to the driver ahead?</u> Feel

The Careless Driver

that tailgating is not that big of a deal that much. In New York it's more prevalent. You used a term tailgating, now that's a technical term in traffic regulations. It's when a driver's vehicle is practically within a yard (36 inches) of the vehicle in front. I'm talking about just following a car length or less than a car length behind at 60/70 mph. Have you seen that in Chicago? Well one, I would say rarely are you driving that fast...rarely not in traffic (garbled). I don't drive on the Interstate that much. That could be it. Let's scratch that question. Here's something you know about. You know that you can use your gears to speed up and to slow down the car, right? Yes. How often do you think you do that? Well, I don't drive a manual anymore, but when I did, I would say that is probably...highway driving?.80% of my slowdowns. Oh, really?! Yeah. Really, 80%--driving on a non-rush-hour basis? Yeah. REALLY? My dad told me that's what you do. Yeah, you can! My dad was always about you shouldn't use your brakes on the Interstate. Oh, I should have met your dad! It's exactly my philosophy. Yeah. Did you know that at one time race cars didn't have brakes?[8] (She didn't know that.)
How often have you seen drivers stopping on the Interstate on-ramp merge lane instead of smoothly merging? Way too often. It should never happen. All right how about changing lanes abruptly? All the

---

[8] 1921 approximately, race cars were outfitted with brakes.

time. (Inaudible.) What about slowing down to view an accident, especially on the other side of the Interstate? That's how you get most traffic jams. Have you seen left hand turners turn too early into the oncoming traffic—this would be on surface streets? That one doesn't jump out at me. How about drivers at a red light have their turn signals on (no cross traffic coming) and they wait and wait? Chicago, most streets are no turn on right, and streets that aren't that way tend to be pretty heavily populated with foot traffic. So, there's not a lot of opportunity to see someone turn on right. All right, going back to my first question: did you get any training from your dad more than when he took you around the parking lot— like from either high school instructors or professional instructors? No, just my parents. (Paused and then ended recording.)

The Careless Driver

The Careless Driver

<u>Interview
Patrick (Rwanda)</u>

The Careless Driver

The Careless Driver

We're in the car with Patrick, whose true home is Rwanda, East Africa, and he did get a license when he was in California about ten years ago. How does a citizen of Rwanda get a license to drive? The training is very tough. You must pass a written test, which is also tough. What are some of the things you are tested on as a driver behind the wheel with a tester or instructor? It's mostly the basic ones the ones that ...but the problem in Rwanda is you have easy roads, small roads, you have so many people working, so it is really rough. Do you have fast moving interstates, like we do? Unfortunately, no. But that is one of the reasons it's really difficult to drive there. Sometimes we bump into people and so if you are taking driving license then you fail. So, in the testing you go on small roads, big roads and paved roads, obviously, But not anything major, no major 70 mph Interstate, okay. Oh, also roads where there are workers. How about in the rain, do they take you out in the rain—test on how you handle a slippery road? I try to do it. In Rwanda you have a long season of rain. So, it's not surprising that you might be taking the test during the rainy season. Now, is this the test or is this the instructing you have to pay for from a professional driver? You have to pay a professional driver to teach you. And now, it's prior to going to the school. Do you think this is now true, even though it's been ten years or more since you were there? I think it's true.

The Careless Driver

Good, I wanted to establish that so as not to give out stale dated or now false information—did your father or mother begin teaching you a little about driving when you were younger? No, I learned how to drive when I was older. When I was eighteen years old. It was an interesting phase. I was very cautious. I didn't have the teenage vibe when I was learning how to drive so as an adult you don't do that. You are very aware of your...So you didn't get a learner's permit like a lot of kids do at sixteen and seventeen? No, I didn't do that. What about-did any of your friends try and teach you who already had licenses who were maybe a little older? Yes, yes.

Okay, how did that go? It went well, yeah. When I took my driving test, I actually did have friends taking them too in a shopping center, big parking lot... You didn't get any training from a professional? That was in California. Let's go back to Rwanda—in Rwanda you had no training whatsoever. No. Okay, it's only when you got to California, and you already graduated high school or college? That is correct. And these were your friends who are also from Rwanda, or from America? From America. Ah, OK, they were in school with you. Now it's clear. So, they said, "Hey, here is Patrick, he's from another country, let's get him a license because he's a nice guy and we like him, and we want to go out with him and have fun. And Patrick said, "Hey, that's a great idea, how about teaching me

The Careless Driver

in the parking lot. So, that's how that happened? That's how we (garbled but essentially "yes"). And after that, no professional training and no school training from college or from anything like that? No.

Then, when you went to get your license in California, which I have also done—I have had a CA license, how did that go? It went really well. As I said, I was very cautious. And what did they ask you to do in California? They take you on a commercial highway. Then they ask you to essentially see how you drive and merge. There are so many California highways you gotta learn how to merge. I took my driver's test on a rainy day, so it was testing my (garbled but essentially "yes"). They took you out on a rainy day? You know why that is—it's so rare to rain in California...(joke)(chuckles). I was so afraid that I was going faster. I was under the speed limit. Oh yeah, so you stayed under the speed limit and did really well. Did they ask you to back up a distance? Yeah. They don't ask you to do that here (in Nashville), backup 10 or 15 feet. All right, merge onto the highway, travel at least one exit, get off, backup, park? Yeah. In the rain? Yeah. Yeah, in the rain, that's great! California, that's better. Some of the northern states are very particular, very tight—very strict, because of the snow they get, as in Illinois, Wisconsin, New Hampshire. There's no program around when I got to Nashville. Well, I found out from people from New Hampshire,

117

Wisconsin and Illinois—some of them go through 40 hours of professional/formal training. They have safe driving. They better, because that's what they are going to be up against six months out of the year.

That's great Patrick, good news. This is about Rwanda, because I wanted to included other countries to show how we fare here, not just in Nashville, but I want to have a local and a regional and a national look at how much training people get: where they get it, when they get it, and where are the deficient areas. Pinpoint the deficient areas. Then just give that data to the public in the book and let others cogitate on that and figure out what they have to [do]: go into a big conference or they have to write their senators and so forth. I'm not going to do that for them. I'm solely presenting the data, which is in no small measure available via the Internet: how many deaths, how many collisions there are on a daily, weekly, yearly basis. But that doesn't tell the story to why that happens. What tells the story is what you are telling me in this interview. (And many others, from Nashville, Wisconsin and from Connecticut New Hampshire, Illinois and from California tell me.)

(On July 17th, 2017 I passed two drivers in the fast lane of the Interstate within a minute or two of each other that were talking on a cell phone and going slower than the traffic in any of the other lanes. I repeat,

The Careless Driver

talking while holding a cell phone,[9] which is of course a distraction, and it seemed making them go slower—like they're being more careful, when they should be going <u>faster,</u> and not talking or at least faster than the other lanes to the right. That as we see posted so often IS THE LAW. In Tennessee slower moving traffic must move over to the right.)

Here then are some sobering facts about roadway fatalities and injuries, for those who can and will read them with a view to applying the information for real to their driving practices:
(From one of my Driver Education Manuals of 2006, *Alabama Safety Institute*, Driver Education Course)
Note: similar statistics, in the main exist for the majority of states, and though dated 2006, the statistics, if at all, are relatively higher for recent years.
Just the sheer number of deaths and injuries should tell us something is amiss definitely and needs re-evaluation towards training and education of drivers, universally. When we see that there are *accident prone*[10] drivers on the road driving, and there are a percentage of drivers who elect *unwisely* a fatal collision as a method of solving a life or relationship gone wrong, we are still left with the overwhelming

---

[9] As of 2021 this practice/habit of talking while holding a cell phone is forbidden by law.
[10] Accident Prone: one who causes accidents in his/her vicinity, sometimes by their mere presence.

evidence that all drivers need to be better trained, and that even well-trained drivers need to continue their education and training as well. Nothing remains in a constant state for long.

For Alabama, 2006 (In summary)
Persons Killed 1,208 up from previous year, 2005 by 5.2 %
Person Injured 43,028 down from previous year, 2005 by 2.6%
Reported Crashes 139,731 down from previous year, 2005 by 2.9%
Miles Traveled 60,394,000,000 up from previous year, 2005 by 1.2%

For myself, the *Miles Traveled* and *Reported Crashes* are very much secondary statistics. But the other two are horrendous for even an entire state: when we consider that the bulk of humanity in that state, the total driving population *minus the drivers injured and killed* far outweigh in numbers the killed and injured. How, we must ask ourselves can so many avoid collisions, but a much smaller percentage don't? This is the effective question that needs to be asked and answered truthfully.

There is a motorcycle training school in Southern California that well trains motorcyclists to confront and successfully handle every possible scenario that can occur on roadways. The success of this school and its graduates is unimpeachable. It has been in existence more than thirty years. If motorcyclists can be educated and trained with this much success, knowing that they are three to five times more vulnerable than automobile drivers shouldn't we be able to formulate the *correct* teaching methods and training to achieve even better results for drivers of cars and SUVs?

Deaths occur in *fatal collisions.* But if there were no, or greatly reduced collisions then there would be greatly reduced *fatalities and injuries. Is this not evident?*

So, the emphasis I see and I champion is to get drivers to get and hone the skills of driving so as to never collide with a person, animal or solid object.

One night as the rain began lightly to fall in Los Angeles I rode out on my motorcycle. I went through a yellow light but then could not avoid a pick-up truck that simply drove out of a gas station without looking or stopping 50 feet on the other side into my right-hand lane. Had I gone to and been trained at the *California Superbike School* I would have laid down the bike and skidded around the truck saving myself a compound fractured right leg and a fractured orbital (eye) socket, two days in intensive care, $22,000.00 in medical costs and six months in a cast that was *very uncomfortable*—not to mention losing those months of *earned* income. In the many years since I have not collided with any person, animal or solid object, although one vehicle has collided with my vehicle, (side-swiped) non-seriously but yet costly in terms of repair costs.

◆◆◆

It is well worth noting as did a master educator once did: that there are people who can drive on the road and there are people driving on roadways who can't drive.* What we can conclude is that steps must be taken to get <u>those persons to join the ranks of the others who can drive</u>. Just to be sure when we say can't drive, we mean the person cannot control a vehicle, which takes them out of the class of *driver,* and puts them in the class of *murderer.* (Potential and real.)

* Not just DUI drivers.

The DUI Driver
(How To Remedy)

The way it's going to happen: the particulars have to be part of the case in front of the judge. If it is not, when the DUI driver gets to the training academy the instructor goes over the whole scenario, finds out what the driver was doing before they drove off and got into a crash or were arrested for DUI. Find out the particulars and replicate the scenario. For example: if the DUI driver was at a party and they were stumbling out of the front door looking for their keys, the instructor does the same thing. Instead of getting in the car, he calls to a friend, "Would someone please drive me home," or "Would you call an Uber or Lyft for me?" Then have the offending DUI driver act out the same scenario with sincerity, motion for motion, word for word or almost verbatim. Instructed without critical remarks or demeaning looks by the instructor. The scenario could be altered if there is more than one DUI conviction and drilled until the DUI student can do it with a straight face calmly. Its role playing to accustom a driver who has made a serious blunder to automatically choose the pro-survival method of getting home. This <u>training</u> is done with a sober supportive attitude if it is to succeed. The DUI driver must act with sincerity or he is not passed by the instructor. Any emotional flashback or joker-degrader comments by the DUI driver is met with a "Do It As Demonstrated." There is no reasoning with the recalcitrant student, because they are below understanding until they can replicate the correct method. THEN, they are in a position to understand why it is the correct way, and why it should be done that way. It may take in some cases several guided run-throughs of one scenario and/or a combination of run-throughs if the DUI student has been convicted of multiple DUI violations.

<u>The attitude towards the student DUI driver is paramount</u>. The DUI driver must perceive that they are in a "learning" position not a disciplinary one. That has already been established by court room appearances, fines and attorney fees. Let the DUI student "blow off steam," if it occurs. It is normal to feel compunction for endangering or injuring the lives of others; but it won't come *usually* without some explosive emotion beforehand. Let the emotional confusion blow off and it will subside. The DUI student will have a realization as well. And that is the guarantee that DUI driving for that student has come to a final end.

We would be wise to also follow this pattern of re-education, refamiliarization of the responsibilities of drivers who are cited and found guilty of texting while driving. The very fact of forming and sending a text

The Careless Driver

message while driving is not itself an immediate censure, if it is done in the following manner: I place my cell phone in a dock attached firmly to the left most area of the windshield just below eye level. And, <u>then</u> I use the facility of dictating a message while I am looking straight ahead at the traffic thus:

Never do we permit fingers to be texting, or to allow drivers to *verbally* text in any other position that obstructs their vision from the traffic in and around them as they are traveling in a vehicle.

Of course, the ideal scenario is this, or the driver has a blue tooth set-up whereby they can dictate, hands free, commands and messages via that device while keeping their eyes focused ahead.

Another scenario for academy driving instructors that has a texting while driving violator to instruct: simply have them in the car, then you have them: the scenario would be you text them using a picture of their boyfriend or girlfriend as it applies and get them to not respond and keep driving or pull off the road and stop. Drill that repetitively however many times it takes until that particular skill is inculcated and indoctrinated properly to a result.

This method (DUI and texting while driving) of getting a more permanent resolution to a driver's poor performance while driving can be applied to any mistake or violation not only DUI or texting thus:

This is how driver training would proceed, for Driving Academies that employ this method of handling moving violations: the instructor welcomes a driver, and proceeds to put them in the passenger seat next

The Careless Driver

to himself in the driver's seat. Instructor has a copy of the court order with the citation number and description of violation. Let's say it is for illegal right-hand turn—turning while left hand vehicles turn from the opposite direction turning into the two lanes, one of which the Violator later turned into causing a collision or the vehicle opposite to yield. The instructor goes to a similar intersection and makes a legal and safe turn into the nearest right-hand lane of the two-lane street. Instructor doesn't say anything to the student. He simply demonstrates the correct method. Now, it is the turn of the person sitting in the passenger seat to get behind the wheel of the instructor's or student's (preferred) vehicle and performs the same maneuver as the instructor moments ago. If the student driver violator does the turn correctly and safely, the instructor tells the student that that is the correct method and in fact he tells the person well done. However, if the student driver does something different than a legal, safe right turn. The driver instructor says, "Let's switch seats again" and proceeds to drive student to a similar intersection, usually the same one and does a legal safe right hand turn, with or without opposing traffic flowing into the right two lanes. Repetition is needed not criticism, nor evaluating the driver's ability. We all learn best with good results when we are shown the proper method. The student changes seats with instructor and proceeds as before to a similar intersection with instructor beside and demonstrates the correct safe right hand turn. Now, the instructor consults the student violator's understanding of why it is the correct method and what can and does happen when it is done illegally.

<u>To go over the theory before showing the correct method and getting that person to do it correctly is to make the same mistake as got them into traffic court to begin with.</u> *They didn't get the rule the first time and or they were taught incorrectly by another driver who also should do this clinic.*

SUMMATION & CONCLUSION

The Careless Driver

The Careless Driver

Summation:

Here's an observation many may have overlooked. On an eight-lane highway (four lanes going each direction) there are only six *useable* lanes, in reality. Why? Notice that the tractor-trailer drivers stay in the next to right most lane. Reason? To avoid having to move back over to that same lane each time another vehicle slower moving at first attempts to merge with the lane they would be traveling in, if they remained in that outer right lane. This is much more the case in rush hour traffic within city limits as the exits are close together and the occurrence of merging and exiting traffic more pronounced. Also, this:
Why is the innermost lane considered the *fast lane, and is designated the passing lane?* Elementary. Almost all exits on fast moving highways (Interstates) begin on the right lane next to the shoulder. This right-most lane then is the lane for slowing down to exit. Consequently, the lane left of that lane is moving faster by default. Expand this into a three or four lane (going one-direction) highway and it is evident that the lanes cooperate with each other to allow slower moving vehicles to move to the lane to the immediate right. And, in many States, this is made a state law and is posted frequently on Interstates along the roadway. The fastest lane is the one where there would be no exits, except in rare occasions, the farthest left lane. This lane is designed and there for

passing slower moving vehicles. <u>Not for traveling in for a great distance as we often see.</u> Otherwise, we get the scenario where a driver passes on the right, the slower moving traffic and causes that lane to divert or slow down as he or she barges in at a faster speed. *This practice is also one of the main causes of rush hour slow-down and delays, i.e. a driver without much notice or insufficient notice decides to "get around" another slower or slowing driver and starts a chain reaction winding up all of the lanes in his direction suddenly braking.*

<u>Conclusion,</u> mine: other countries do and require more professional training than the U.S. Consequently, they have lower per capita death rates and lower injury rates—even with more strenuous road circumstances, ex: Rwanda, Philippines. We pay a tremendous amount of dollars annually for auto insurance in the United States. **What would happen if a small fraction of the billions spent on auto insurance and hospitalization was spent per capita (per driver) on professional driver training?**
Our states could mandate that *instead of sending traffic violators and accident causing drivers to traffic school,* <u>*they are ordered to driver training classes, and*</u> **<u>shown how to do correctly what they failed to do—and passed only when they do it as well.</u>** I don't believe joy of causing pain is the reason we go out and get stinking drunk and then drive our vehicle into

another one, mangling the bodies of those therein, nor the reason we speed down poorly lit highways and roads at speed limit plus 40 mph to the result of unrecognizable wrecking yard debris. No, I believe we do these things simply because our ability to create a life for oneself has gone astray so badly that the only solution is to <u>try to</u> uncreate it with force. Notice, *try to* underlined. It never quite uncreates it.

But this work is not aimed at that segment of motorists described above anyway. They are another *different problem,* different than the one this work intends to quell.

Today September 15, 2017, I was reminded by a woman from the United Kingdom of another annoying, unnecessary driver fault: turning out or left to turn right at a corner or driveway. This she reveals is maddening, and I'll add to that that it causes unnecessary stoppage and or stress on drivers behind who do not predict what is going to happen. This phenomenon is widespread and not indigenous to Tennessee drivers. The main type of vehicle and driver seen doing this *habitually* is the SUV. My concept and *recommendation:* Take the turn slower or if it is a driveway go over the curb, it isn't going to damage an SUV, unless there is a culvert that a narrow driveway *bridge* is used to span it. That's an uncommon situation with most driveways.

The Careless Driver

And one of my irritations on surface streets: a driver comes to a stop for a jaywalking pedestrian, coming from the other direction traffic lanes: already putting himself in danger. No driver cognizance of vehicles behind, just stops, and in sight of a well painted crosswalk the pedestrian could see and should have used.

It is or should be of interest to all drivers to take note that a typical SUV in the United States weighs *in excess of 1 and a half to twice the weight of a passenger car.* For example, the Nissan *Armada,* comes in at a whopping 7,500 lbs. A Nissan *Altima,* weighs at maximum 3,342 lbs. Get where were going with this? If an SUV driver continues to <u>only use the brakes but not gain the skill to also use the gears to slow the vehicle down, not only will there be additional unnecessary brake repairs, there will be an unending scenario on highways and roadways of seeing these motor vehicle's (and other's) stop lights go on unnecessarily over and over again and of course crashes to car rear end or worse.</u>

Also, choosing the right gear to travel in <u>improves fuel efficiency</u>—something all drivers have a vested interest in.

Final Conclusion: If we as a nation were to adopt a standard of driver training much like Mr. Pitner offers, with a minimum of 30 hours of professional driver training, with more rigorous testing before granting license, we would see in a short period of time a dwindling of *accidents*, and the resultant carnage and wreckage we have become inured of over the years. That is the hope and future look of this work.

As a final footnote, it is no coincidence that the states with the highest number of hours of supervised driver training, HAW, MA, MD, NH, NJ, have the lowest per capita vehicle fatality rates of all 50 states.
Their relative per capita ratio of vehicular deaths to population, 2016:
HAW   109/1,400,000=   0.000078   or   0.008%
MA   359/6,800,000=   0.005%
MD   477/6,000,000=   0.008%
NH   130/1,340,000=   0.009%
NJ   569/8,900,000=   0.006%

States (as example) with minor supervised training requirements:
TX   3,407/27,800,000=   0.012%
FL   2,933/20,600,00=   0.014%

Statistic: More than 25% of teen fatalities on highways are caused by teens in rear seat distracting driver. Shouldn't we be drilling young drivers to pull off road,

The Careless Driver

stop the car and exit the boisterous teens? Shouldn't this be as a matter of rule in driving school (high school, professional) courses a mandatory requirement? 58% are distracted teens (all distractions counted) Source: *National Organizations For Teen Safety.*

Curious fact: there is a 10-minute test that identifies *accident prone* individuals that are the cause of many highway collisions, outside of but not necessarily exclusive of DUI drivers. Shouldn't we d*emand* that this test be administered to all applicants for driving privileges? We go to great lengths to guard against terrorists boarding U.S. commercial planes and other conveyances, government buildings, court houses etc. why can we not demand and screen those that would cause deadly accidents?

Don't just drive defensively, drive *expertly.* Fare thee well.

The Careless Driver

PROPOSED LEGISLATION BASED ON THE RESEARCH

TITLE OF BILL: SENIOR DRIVER CAPABILITY ASSURANCE ACT

BE IT ENACTED BY THE TENNESSEE CONGRESS

Preamble: WHEREAS, current Tennessee statutes concerning driver license renewals allow for a 8-year period with automatic renewal by mail or online, and WHEREAS this practice can permit and has permitted senior citizens with lessened driving capability to drive on our highways and streets, and WHEREAS this existing renewal system allows therefore non-optimum individual drivers to be a liability on our roadways, unbeknownst to other drivers,

SECTION 1: This act may be cited as the "Senior Driver Capability Assurance Bill."

SECTION 2: Seniors, 60 years or older are required to pass a vision, and hearing test every 3 years to obtain/retain driving privileges.

> Sub-SECTION A: Seniors, 60 years or older who have been involved in vehicle, pedestrian, or animal collision within the past 3 years are required to pass a vision, hearing and reflex test to obtain/retain driving privileges. Note: provision for these additional tests are already covered under, 55-50-322 (a) (1) (A) but are made mandatory with this bill for seniors 60 years and older.
>
> Sub-SECTION B: Statute 55-50-322 (b) (1)* is amended to read: In the case of a non-resident 60 years of age or older, applying for a Tennessee

The Careless Driver

driver's license, they must submit to a vision and hearing test, as well as a reflex test if they have been in a collision with another person, animal, or vehicle within the past 3 years.

Sub-SECTION C: that this bill amends also T50-322-50-322 (I) (2) (B) wherein a foreign country driver age 60 or older must submit to the same eye and hearing tests as a resident 60 years or older, and the reflex test if they also have been in a collision with a person, vehicle or animal within the past 3 years. Note: 55-50-303 (a) (5) does not need to be amended since that provision does not specify a *written* examination.

Sub-SECTION D: That a neighbor by way of personal repeated observations, may, as well as a family member or health care professional, make a report of an elderly unsafe driver to The Tennessee Department of Safety Driver Improvement Section, provided they have first informed the family of the elderly person with whom that elderly person lives, or the elderly person themselves, if that person lives alone.

SECTION 3: This bill shall go into effect 91 days after passage.

*55-50-322 (B) (1) THE DEPARTMENT MAY WAIVE THE REQUIRED KNOWLEDGE AND SKILLS TESTS UPON APPLICATION FOR A TENNESSEE DRIVER LICENSE BY A NONRESIDENT WHO ESTABLISHES RESIDENCY IN THIS STATE. THE NEW RESIDENT MUST SURRENDER A DRIVER LICENSE OR SUBMIT A CERTIFIED REPORT FROM THE FORMER STATE OF RESIDENCE. EITHER THE LICENSE OR THE REPORT SHALL

VERIFY THAT THE LICENSE IS NOT SUBJECT TO CANCELLATION, SUSPENSION OR REVOCATION AND THAT THE LICENSE IS VALID, OR HAS NOT BEEN EXPIRED IN EXCESS OF SIX (6) MONTHS.

The Careless Driver

The Careless Driver

Title of Bill: Tennessee Driver's Road Test Improvement Bill

BE IT ENACTED BY THE TENNESSEE CONGRESS

Preamble: WHEREAS, current Tennessee road tests are inadequate to the demands of our daily Interstate and highway traffic, and whereas a new applicant for driver's license is only asked to go the speed limit, stop at stop signs and make four legal right turns in order to pass, and whereas 94% of all serious crashes are due to driver error. NHSTA (2019). Whereas current TN road tests for new driver's should but doesn't demand skills necessary to navigate Tennessee Interstates and back roads successfully without collisions. Whereas the fatalities on Tennessee roadways has essentially and steadily increased over the past six years, when they should be declining due to state and local police and safety organizations efforts but are yet at an unacceptable level. The statistics are 2014/963; 2015/962; 2016/1014; 2017/1037; 2018/1041 deaths on Tennessee roadways. Whereas from survey of 100 plus Tennessee drivers in 2019 the main complaint of their fellow drivers is the poor lane changing and no or inadequate signaling that drivers demonstrate continuously, followed by excessive speed and, whereas many northern states with fewer fatalities than TN road test their drivers requiring demonstration by applicant of far more skills than Tennessee's requirements the following should be made Tennessee statutes.

SECTION 1: This act may be cited as the "Tennessee Driver's Road Test Improvement Bill."

SECTION 2:

Sub-SECTION A: A suitable *minimum* road test should include the following (From the 2006 AL Driver Education Course*): <u>After examiner makes all vehicle checks:</u>

Proper Signaling (Giving cars behind and to either side, if it applies, sufficient clicks of the signal: usually three).
Lane changing both left and right.
Right and left turns and a U-turn.
Use of marked and unmarked lanes of traffic.
Backing of vehicle (In Wisconsin / Utah 30-50 foot and100 foot back up smoothly required respectively).
Making a quick stop.
Observance of traffic signs and signals.
General control of vehicle.
Observation
Three point turn. *With turn signals.* Stop vehicle at right side of curb. Viz, When safe make a sharp left turn, back vehicle. Move forward in right lane. Do not bump curb or use driveway.
Parking (uphill <u>and</u> downhill)
*And Utah Driver's Road Test 2014

<u>Sub-SECTION B:</u>
<u>SECTION 3</u>: This bill shall go into effect 91 days after passage.

The Careless Driver

Title of Bill: Tennessee Vehicle Operator's Retraining Program Bill

BE IT ENACTED BY THE TENNESSEE CONGRESS

Preamble: WHEREAS, current Tennessee statutes concerning driving school permits convicted moving violators to option for 'traffic school' if no earlier conviction on their driving record exists in a prior 12 month period, and WHEREAS, major moving violators can avoid points and increased insurance rates by taking this option, and WHEREAS this practice can permit and has permitted serious offenders—those whose offense could have injured or killed one or more persons, to avoid permanent remedial actions in contrast to verbal traffic school lectures, and WHEREAS this existing option system allows therefore non-optimum individual drivers to be a liability on our roadways,

SECTION 1: This act may be cited as the "Tennessee Vehicle Operator's Retraining Program Bill."

SECTION 2: Major moving vehicle violators, such as speeding in a work zone, running red lights or running stop signs, overtaking and passing school, youth or church bus, reckless driving are remanded to this program.

> Sub-SECTION A: Any convicted moving vehicle violator comes under and is remanded to this vehicle operator retraining program who commits a traffic violation of four (4) points or more.

> Sub-SECTION B: The convicted moving

143

vehicle violator is remanded to either a PD or private Driving Academy, with the full particulars of the offense transmitted in duplicate, one copy for the Driving Academy, one for the violator who becomes a student in the retraining program. Note: Often the violator will have never had any formal training much less professional training in how to control and drive a motor vehicle. And, although in some instances the student may exhibit bad emotion, such as protest, or anger to begin with at being carefully instructed, same student will not pass until without said protest, justification or alibi for the convicted offense the student performs the action according to best driving principles and the extant law, and, *more importantly shows a new understanding to the instructor as to why the law exists.*

Sub-SECTION C: It is vital to note that in cases such as DWI and texting while driving that a student may protest, sometimes loudly, knowing in truth that they could have caused death or irreparable bodily injury to another by their carelessness and this must be dealt with in a firm but not accusative manner by the instructor assigned to the student. But that no student may be passed in a state of mind whereby they glibly do the action they failed to perform or that continue to exhibit protest, justification or alibi for their mistakes.

Sub-SECTION D: When a student so remanded to professional driver retraining has honestly and successfully passed, they can apply to the court of jurisdiction for the waiving of the sentence so as not to accumulate the points, and this is done in a conciliatory inducement to the student to obey the law from here on, with the proviso that if they are cited and convicted within a 3-year period for the same or similar offense then they not only pay all fines and costs of courts, but they also have the points waived as well as the new points go against their driving record.

Sub-SECTION E: In accordance with TN 55-10-301, (b) (1) (C) (2) the fees for this driver retraining program should not exceed those given in the above cited sub-chapter, including the verbiage for inability to pay with an amendment to 55-10-301, (b) (1) (C) (2) allowing for this bill's fee schedule to be the similar.

SECTION 3: This bill shall go into effect 91 days after passage.

The Careless Driver

APPENDIX

Can you estimate which answer was the most chosen?

Yes.

Can you also come up with the main complaint (negative sentiment) of the survey?

Abrupt lane changing (into their vehicle's path)

The Careless Driver

Acknowledgement

Lyn Cianflocco:
National Highway Traffic Safety Administration-
National Center for Statistics & Analysis Data
Reporting & Information Division

Sean Pitner - Pitner Driving School

The 26 passenger/riders who contributed their stories to the original book The Careless Driver

The Careless Driver

About the Author

Van Heyden has been writing and publishing his works for the past 15 years. He loves children, loves pets, especially retrievers and Dalmatians. He's a big fan of and plays tennis well. Likes fast cars. Likes wooded residential environments., and loves winding roads that disappear to seemingly nowhere-and explores them. Loves researching strange topics and coming up with unusual or little known facts about people and events. Can be found to supply the correct 'phrase' or saying for the misquoted one. And he plays a good game of 'Trivia' (not the game so much as the exercise verbally with his passenger/riders when he is professionally chauffeuring them. He won't stop writing for a long time to come, and he won't be going to the Great Beyond anytime soon; in fact it may be longer than most can comfortably imagine.

The Careless Driver

The Careless Driver

Look for How To Stay Healthy Until We Die, a primer for youth so they can enjoy a healthier life when they attain adulthood.

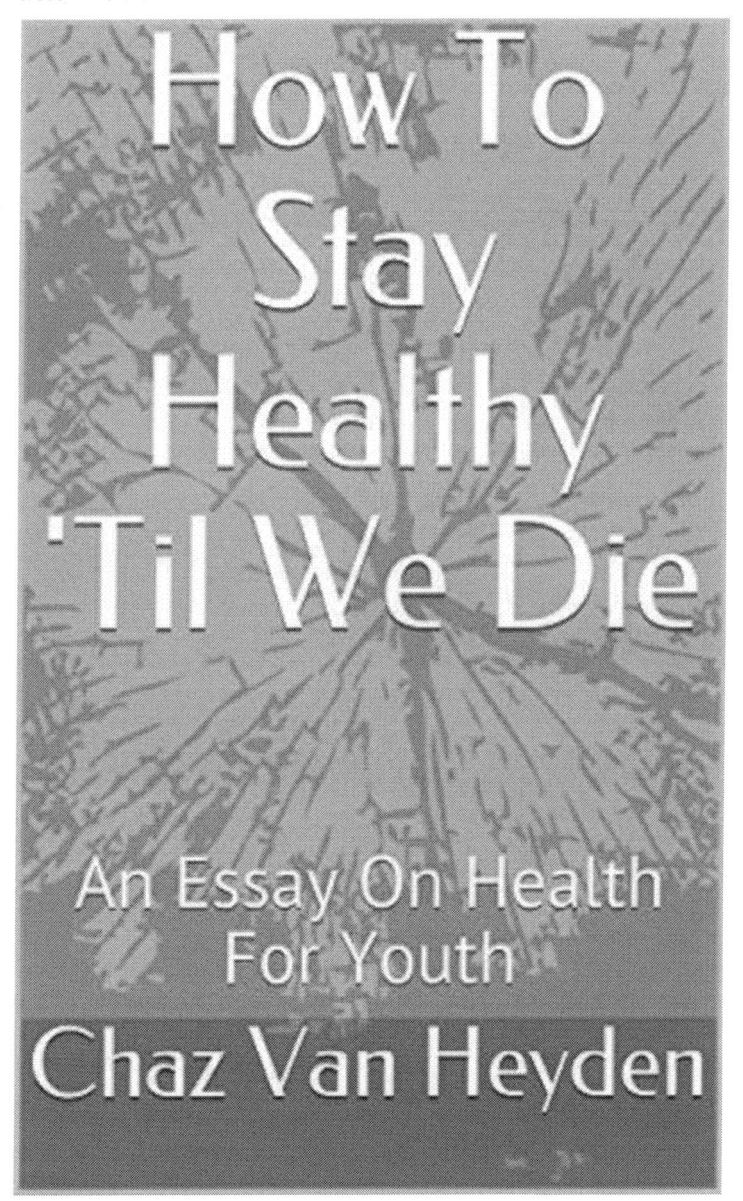

How To Stay Healthy 'Til We Die

An Essay On Health For Youth

Chaz Van Heyden

The Careless Driver

The Careless Driver

From The Publisher

To reach the author with comments and/or questions please send a SASE with your letter to :

VG Publishing
83 Jay Street
Nashville, TN, 37210
Attention: Publisher-Frank A. Carlyle

Alternately via

facarlyle@vgpublishing.org
Campaign: vgpublishing.org/campaign

Made in the USA
Columbia, SC
15 November 2024

4f99bf70-f5ce-401f-9d79-0a6b35da1db4R01